sew your own
scandi
wardrobe

ODA STORMOEN
KRISTIN VAAG

Photography by Ida Bjørvik

Hardie Grant

QUADRILLE

Contents

Preface

Sewing is a craft of long-standing traditions. Looking back, the sewing machine was a fixture in every home, and sewing skills were passed down from generation to generation. The latest fashion from Paris was beyond reach for most, and women used their sewing machines to create their own fashion. We are thrilled to be experiencing a true resurgence in the interest for sewing, especially at a time where the latest fashion is just a click away. Sewing your own clothes is a wonderful counterbalance to the industrialized ways of 'fast fashion', promoting both social and environmental responsibility whilst providing a wonderful arena for personal expression.

By creating, designing, and sewing your own clothes, you not only get to explore your creativity and make something uniquely your own, but you can also feel good knowing that you are consuming fashion in a more sustainable and conscious manner. We believe that, through learning how to sew, you gain important knowledge about the work and care that is required to create each and every garment, and the importance of respecting the craftsmanship it represents.

Through this book, we want to bring the joy of sewing and creation to the next level by combining the traditional with the modern. We've created patterns for clothes that are just as beautiful, contemporary and appealing as those you'll find in a store. We also want to give everyone the opportunity to unleash their inner designer, by being able to customize the designs to their own style and liking. This book provides the tools you need to create an entire wardrobe of fantastic, self-sewn clothes that are unique to you. The goal is for you to be able to sew cherished pieces that will last for years to come, that can be styled in wide variety of ways, adapted to your preferences, and remain just as relevant and desirable in the future as today.

We set out to create the book we've been missing in our own sewing rooms, complete with patterns, techniques, and proper guidance for achieving great results when sewing. In the first section, you'll learn about good habits, preparation, and how to make conscious fabric choices. In the next section you'll find patterns for 18 essential and classic garments and accessories that will elevate any wardrobe. In the last section, you'll find an overview of all the sewing techniques and variations that we refer to in the patterns, and that you will find useful for future projects beyond this book as well. We hope you find the book inspiring, and that it will follow you as a faithful companion on your sewing journey from here.

We would love to see what you create! Use the hashtag #sewscandi on Instagram to share your makes and inspire others with your creativity.

All the best,
Oda and Kristin

Overview of the garments

The book features a collection of designs that together make up what we believe is a complete basic wardrobe, including key garments and accessories that can be used all year round. The designs complement each other, allowing for endless mix and match possibilities and versatility in creating outfits suitable for both everyday wear and special occasions. Our goal is for these to become timeless wardrobe favourites, cherished for their longevity and ability to be worn repeatedly. We understand that style and preferences are personal, which is why we have included several variations for each project allowing you to create the garment that is perfect for your individual style.

- Turtleneck sweater
- Blouse
- Shirt
- Crewneck
- T-shirt
- Blazer
- Coat
- Straight skirt
- Wrap skirt
- Trousers
- Everyday dress
- Wrap dress
- Babydoll dress
- Cocktail dress
- Jumpsuit
- Swimsuit
- Baguette bag
- Beret

The pattern sheets

This book includes PDF pattern sheets, which can be downloaded at www.hardiegrant.com/uk/quadrille/scandi-wardrobe. The base patterns can be used to sew a variety of different garments and be combined in different ways. For instance, the straight top can be lengthened to make the everyday dress, and the fitted top can be combined with the skirt and extended to make the wrap dress, or combined with the trousers to make the jumpsuit. The sewing instructions describe which pieces are needed for the specific garment. We also provide guidance on how to modify the pattern pieces, with variations such as different sleeve styles, necklines, collars and lengths. You will find detailed instructions for these variations on pages 197–221.

Each pattern piece is graded in sizes, and the pattern sheets feature colour-coded lines for each size. To create the pattern pieces in your size, simply place a semi-transparent paper over the pattern sheet and trace the relevant lines. All pattern pieces include a 1 cm (⅜ in) seam allowance.

Pattern pieces

Straight top:	front piece, back piece, sleeve, shirt collar
Fitted top:	front piece, back piece, sleeve
Jacket:	front piece, back piece, collar, sleeve, pocket, pocket flap
Skirt:	front piece, back piece
Trousers:	front piece, back piece
Other pieces:	waistband, cuff, fly facing, fly flap
Swimsuit:	front piece, back piece
Baguette bag:	side piece, bottom, ring tab, handle

Drawing pattern pieces

In some projects you may need to create or adjust specific pattern pieces. This typically involves drawing rectangles based on measurements, or simple pieces based on the existing pieces from the pattern sheets. Additionally there are optional variations that you can draw yourself, such as pockets and decorative collars. These are described in the Variations section on pages 197–221. In each project you will find an illustration with an overview of the pattern pieces needed from the pattern sheets, as well as any pieces you may need to draw or modify. The base pattern is illustrated with a black line. If there is a purple line, this indicates alterations or pieces you need to draw yourself. If a line is dotted, it should not be cut.

Taking measurements

→ *You will find the everyday dress on page 109.*

When taking measurements of yourself, stand in front of a mirror to ensure accuracy. Hold the measuring tape horizontally, and avoid pulling it too tightly. It is also recommended that you wear form-fitting clothing, such as leggings and a tank top. The sizes in the book are based on three key measurements: bust, waist and hip circumference.

To measure your bust, determine the widest part of your chest area and measure around that.

To locate where to take your waist measurement, stand in front of the mirror and bend your upper body to the side. The measurement should be taken where your upper body bends.

For your hip measurement, measure around the widest part of your hips or buttocks. Note that this is usually slightly lower than where the hip is traditionally considered to be.

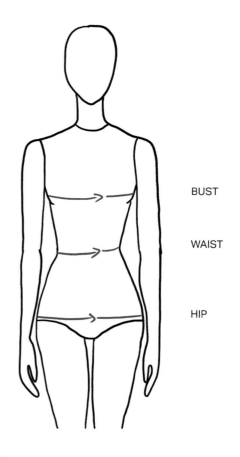

BUST

WAIST

HIP

Sizing guide

The patterns include nine sizes, ranging from UK 6/ US 2/EU 34 to UK 22/US 18/EU 50. The measurement chart below shows which size you should choose based on your body measurements. For some projects you may be advised to select a size that differs from your standard size. This is to achieve the desired appearance of the garment – some designs may call for an oversized look, while others require a more fitted silhouette and are intended to be sewn in stretchy fabric. As a result, some patterns include two additional sizes to accommodate these variations.

European size	-	34	36	38	40	42	44	46	48	50	+
UK size		6	8	10	12	14	16	18	20	22	
US size		2	4	6	8	10	12	14	16	18	
Bust	74 cm (29 in)	80 cm (31½ in)	84 cm (33 in)	88 cm (34½ in)	92 cm (36¼ in)	96 cm (37¾ in)	100 cm (39½ in)	106 cm (41¾ in)	110 cm (43¼ in)	116 cm (45½ in)	120 cm (47¼ in)
Waist	60 cm (23¾ in)	64 cm (25¼ in)	68 cm (26¾ in)	72 cm (28¼ in)	76 cm (30 in)	80 cm (31½ in)	84 cm (33 in)	90 cm (35½ in)	96 cm (37¾ in)	102 cm (40 in)	108 cm (42½ in)
Hips	84 cm (33 in)	88 cm (34½ in)	92 cm (36¼ in)	96 cm (37¾ in)	100 cm (39½ in)	106 cm (41 in)	108 cm (42½ in)	114 cm (45 in)	120 cm (47¼ in)	126 cm (49¾ in)	132 cm (52 in)

← You will find the blazer
  on page 67.

Adjusting the pattern to your size

Few people fit perfectly into one size, and the great thing about sewing your own clothes is that you can adjust the garment to fit your body perfectly.

On the pattern pieces you will find marked lines for the bust, waist and hip, corresponding to where you measured your bust, waist, and hip circumference. For the trousers and skirts, the top edge corresponds to the waist. To adjust the pattern pieces to your measurements, simply draw your own lines between the sizes that fit you best – see illustration.

Before making any adjustments take a good look at pictures of the garment to examine the fit.

An oversized crewneck allows for more flexibility in measurement, while for a fitted dress you should make the necessary adjustments to the pattern beforehand.

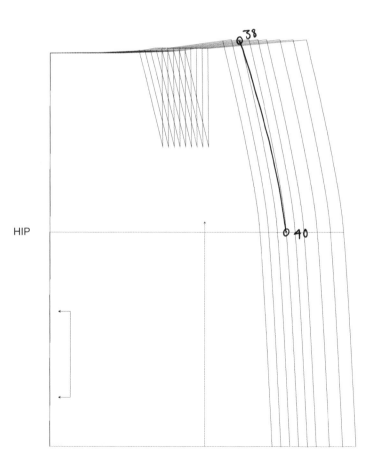

HIP

Preparation and good habits

Thorough preparation is key when it comes to sewing. It can be easy to forget in the eagerness to get started, but proper preparation is nearly half the job in a sewing project. Taking the time to cut, press, mark, and secure raw edges on the fabric pays off immensely. Further work becomes easier and more organized, and this ultimately leads to a much better result.

This is what you need:
- Sewing machine
- Measuring tape
- Good fabric scissors
- Universal scissors for everything that is not fabric
- Pins
- Hand-sewing needles
- Tracing paper
- Ruler
- Tape
- Seam ripper
- Something to mark with (chalk, pen, etc.)
- Iron

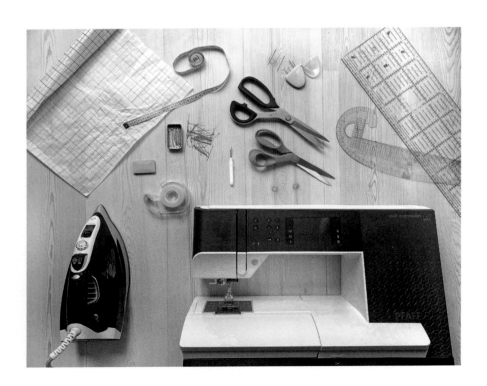

Tracing the pattern

Before you can begin cutting and sewing, it is necessary to transfer the pattern pieces you need onto a suitable material. We recommend tracing paper – a lightweight and partially transparent paper on a roll. Place the tracing paper on the pattern sheet to trace the pieces for the garment you are making. Some people prefer to use builders' plastic or pattern interfacing (not to be confused with fusible/iron-on interfacing).

In many of the projects, you will need to modify the base pattern or draw pattern pieces on your own. When tracing the patterns, work on a flat surface and use heavy objects or pattern weights to keep the pattern paper steady. Copy relevant lines and markings onto the tracing paper, and remember to label the pattern pieces with the name, size, and any adjustments made. By taking good care of the pattern pieces, they can be reused and you won't have to redo the work every time you want to sew something new from the book.

How much fabric do I need?

The book is provided with base patterns and variations to create a range of different garments. You will therefore need to calculate how much fabric each project requires, depending on the choices you make regarding sleeves, length, and other variations. Ideally, start by making the pattern pieces and lay them out to estimate the fabric requirement.

See page 223 for an overview Fabric quantity guide to help you with the calculation. This indicates the fabric requirement for the base patterns found on the pattern sheets. Please note that this overview does not allow for any additional pattern pieces you draw yourself, or any pattern alterations you make. However, it serves as a helpful starting point for your calculations.

Choice of fabric

→ *You will find the coat on page 77, and the beret on page 159.*

We probably don't need to tell you that we have a huge love for fabrics. We can spend hours wandering through fabric stores, immersing ourselves in different textures and possibilities, before deciding on what to use in a project. Not because finding suitable fabric is challenging, but rather because it's difficult to choose between all the fantastic options available. Selecting the right fabric for a project really is the alpha and omega for how it will turn out. That doesn't necessarily mean that there are right or wrong fabrics for each project, but that the fabric plays a big role in the shape and expression of the finished garment. Therefore, it pays to have basic knowledge of how different fabrics behave, how they drape, how they reflect light, and how demanding they are to sew.

The world of fabrics is complicated, and there is no easy way out there to acquire the available knowledge; much of it simply comes with experience. Throughout this book we will do our best to convey the knowledge and preferences we have acquired ourselves. To make the choice a little easier for you we have provided suggestions for suitable fabrics in the instructions for each garment. One thing that can be confusing when talking about fabrics is that the terms for textile materials and fabric quality are often used interchangeably. For instance, cotton, linen, and silk are examples of materials used in a variety of fabric qualities. Satin, denim, and organza are examples of fabric qualities that can be made from different textile materials. Satin, for example, can be woven from cotton, silk, polyester, or similar fibres. Woven fabric qualities in materials such as cotton and linen are very easy to work with for beginners because they are stable and both easy to iron and manage when sewing. Satin and chiffon, on the other hand, require more experience and concentration to finish nicely, because they tend to slip and behave in a more fluid manner.

Fabric guide

Quality	Fabric	Properties	Recommendation
Brocade	Silk, linen, wool, synthetic materials	Heavy, stiff fabric with woven surface pattern often made from gold or silver threads	Cocktail dress Baguette bag
Broderie anglaise	Cotton	Tightly woven cotton fabric with embroidered details and perforated pattern	Dress Blouse
Canvas	Cotton	Heavy fabric. Stiff and prone to wrinkling	Baguette bag
Chiffon	Silk, synthetic materials	Thin, transparent, and easy to drape	Skirt Dress Blouse
Corduroy	Cotton	Woven fabric with vertical velvet stripes. Stripes can be narrow (baby cord) or wide	Skirt Blouse
Crepe	Silk, wool, synthetic materials	Fabric with crinkled surface	Blouse Wrap skirt Trousers Jumpsuit
Cupro	Cupro	Silk-like fabric made from cellulose. Light, soft, and breathable	Dress Skirt Blouse
Denim	Cotton	Heavy-duty cotton twill	Skirt
French terry	Cotton	Sweatshirt fabric. Smooth knitted surface and loops on the reverse	Crewneck
Gobelin	Cotton, synthetic materials	Thick and heavy fabric woven in various motifs and patterns. Often used for interior design	Baguette bag
Faux leather	Often vinyl-coated	Colour and texture reminiscent of leather	Baguette bag
French terry	Cotton	Sweatshirt fabric. Smooth knit surface and brushed reverse. Warm and comfortable	Crewneck
Fusible interfacing	Cotton or cotton/polyester mix	Reinforcement fabric with adhesive on one or both sides	Used to reinforce pattern pieces such as facings and cuffs
Jersey	Cotton	Knitted, stretchy fabric	T-shirt Turtleneck sweater

Quality	Fabric	Properties	Recommendation
Linen	Linen	Creases easily. Cool against the skin	Blouse Skirt Babydoll dress Jumpsuit
Lycra	Synthetic materials	Stretch fabric suitable for sportswear and swimwear	Swimsuit
Muslin	Cotton	Two layers of thin cotton that are woven together. Shrinks when washed and gets a characteristic, crinkled appearance	Dress Blouse
Organza	Silk, synthetic materials	Transparent and glossy	Blouse Dress
Ribbed knit	Cotton	Double-knitted, stretchy fabric. Thicker than regular jersey	T-shirt Crewneck (used as, among other things, neckband and cuffs)
Satin	Cotton, silk, synthetic materials	Smooth and glossy fabric	Lining fabric Blouse Cocktail dress
Thai silk	Silk	Silk fabric with a crinkled surface	Dress Skirt Blouse
Tweed	Wool	Rough woollen fabric with distinctive weaving. Warm	Coat Blazer
Twill	Cotton	Weaving method that gives a diagonal pattern in the fabric	Trousers Coat Blazer
Velvet	Silk, cotton, viscose, synthetic materials	Woven fabric with a fuzzy, shiny, and soft surface on one side	Skirt Cocktail dress Baguette bag
Wool felt	Wool	Soft and thick woollen fabric	Beret
Lightweight woven cotton	Cotton	Durable and breathable	Skirt Dress Blouse
Woven viscose	Viscose	Light and soft fabric. Breathable and comfortable against the skin	Dress Skirt Blouse

← *You will find the blouse on page 41, and the straight skirt on page 87.*

Eco-friendly materials

For many, including ourselves, sustainability is a contributing factor in choosing to sew our own clothes rather than buying new ones in the store. When making your own clothes, you are in control of the production process and creation of the garment itself. However, it is important to consider the sustainability of the materials you choose for your sewing project.

Our recommendation is to prioritize natural plant fibre materials such as linen and cotton, or animal fibres such as silk and wool. When it comes to synthetically produced materials, it is best to avoid oil-based ones such as acrylic and polyester, because they are essentially plastic. However, there are also synthetically produced materials made from plant fibres, such as viscose, lyocell and rayon. These semi-synthetic alternatives do not release microplastics when washed, making them a better choice. You can also look for recycled and organic labelled materials. In addition, always look for environmental certifications such as Oeko-Tex, GOTS, and Bluesign, because they ensure that the fabric meets their stringent environmental and social standards.

Recycled fabrics

Re-using fabrics when sewing is an excellent way to utilize products that have already been produced, which contributes to minimize the environmental impact of textile production. We love to go to flea markets or charity shops in search of secondhand treasures, such as tablecloths, curtains, bedding and bedspreads. However, it is important to pay attention to fabric quality and fibre content and to assess whether the fabric is suitable as a garment. Investing time and effort into sewing a garment only for the weaving to unravel afterwards would be disappointing. Building the experience in identifying suitable secondhand fabrics may involve some trial and error. However, the world is full of used textiles, so don't be discouraged if not every find works out.

It's important to note that there is no need to feel guilty about choosing new fabrics over secondhand if it means achieving better quality and a longer lifespan for the garment. We use a varied mix of new and secondhand fabrics, which works great for us!

Pre-washing fabrics

→ You will find the babydoll dress on page 125.

When purchasing a fabric, it often comes with information about expected shrinkage after washing. It is always advisable to wash the fabric before cutting out the pattern pieces to prevent the finished garment from shrinking the first time you wash it. Also, washing helps to remove any colour residues or other substances that may be present from production. Wash the fabric according to the manufacturer's instructions. If these are not available, wash the fabric in the same manner as you would the finished garment. After washing, allow the fabric to air dry.

Once the fabric is dry, iron it to smooth out wrinkles and inspect it for any flaws. This way, you can avoid areas with defects when cutting out your pattern pieces.

Cutting

When cutting the pattern pieces, first lay the fabric out on a flat surface. Make sure it has no folds or wrinkles, then secure the pattern pieces to the fabric with weights or pins to prevent it moving while you cut. Pay close attention to the cutting instructions for each project. These instructions will specify the number of times you need to cut each piece, which pieces need to be cut on the fold of doubled fabric, and which pieces may need additional interfacing or stabilizing fabric. The cutting instructions will also tell you if any pattern pieces need alterations or to be drawn from scratch before being cut. Each pattern piece has an arrow indicating the direction of the grain, which shows how the pattern pieces should be positioned on the fabric. We recommend folding the fabric in half lengthwise and begin by cutting all the pieces that need to be cut against the fold or in two parts. This also applies when cutting mirrored pattern pieces, for example, a two-piece back.

Grainline: A woven fabric will have threads running vertically and horizontally, these are the grainlines. The vertical threads run parallel to the selvedge of the fabric. To place the pattern pieces correctly, the grainline arrow must be parallel to the selvedge. Note that some pattern pieces are cut on the bias to create elasticity or drape in the fabric. For fabrics that do not have a woven grainline, we still recommend using the selvedge as a starting point for the drape and pattern on the fabric.

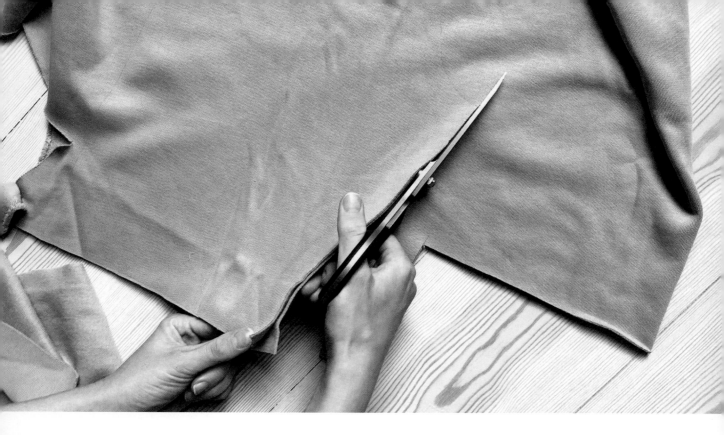

Explanation of cutting instructions

Cut 1   Place the pattern piece on a single layer of fabric and cut out one piece.

Cut 2   Place the pattern piece on a double layer of fabric to cut out two mirrored pattern pieces.

Cut on the fold   Place the pattern piece on a double layer of fabric with the centreline against the fabric fold.

Add seam allowance along the centre line   If the project requires two separate pattern pieces instead of one piece cut on the fold, you will be instructed to add a seam allowance along the centre line. Cut 1 cm (⅜ in) outside the centreline on the pattern, to add extra seam allowance.

Cut in interfacing   The pattern piece should be cut in fusible interfacing to be ironed onto the corresponding fabric piece. You can also iron interfacing onto the fabric before cutting.

Pencil icon: ✎   The pencil icon indicates when a pattern piece needs alterations or to be drawn from scratch before cutting the fabric. Read the instructions carefully and apply the changes to your traced pattern.

Right or wrong side up when cutting?

A question that often arises is whether to cut from the right or wrong side of the fabric. There is no definitive answer, and you can choose which you prefer. The advantage of cutting with the wrong side facing up is that you can more easily make markings on the fabric that will not be visible on the right side. The advantage of cutting with the right side facing up is that it allows for better visibility of the fabric's design, making it easier to decide on pattern placement. Both methods are effective, and you can vary your approach depending on the fabric you are using.

Pattern placement and pattern matching

When working with a fabric that has a design, you need to consider this when laying out the pattern pieces on the fabric. Deciding how the design should sit on the front piece is often a good place to start. There is no definitive right or wrong way to do this, you simply have to consider what you think looks good. When taking fabric design placement into account, you may require more fabric than if you were using a plain-coloured fabric, because you cannot utilize all parts of the fabric in the same way.

If you have chosen a fabric with a repetitive design – such as a plaid – it is crucial to ensure that the design matches across the pattern pieces. It would be visually disturbing if the squares suddenly become offset, particularly in highly visible places such as a front or back seam. To succeed with pattern matching, we recommend first cutting one piece and then using it as a template to cut out the mirrored piece. Place the first piece on the fabric, aligning all the squares, and then carefully cut out the second piece. Taking the time to pin or tack (baste) the squares in place before sewing will help ensure proper alignment during the sewing process.

Marking

The pattern pieces feature elements that need to be marked and transferred onto the fabric. These marks provide information on how the garment should be constructed and can, for example, include notches, darts, pleats, and other details. Clear markings are helpful when sewing the garment, and it is important to transfer them precisely onto the fabric before you start sewing. Keep in mind that the marks should not be visible on the completed garment. Therefore, place them on the wrong side of the fabric, in the seam allowance, or use marking tools such as chalk, water-soluble pen, or thread that can be removed later.

Choose your method based on the fabric you are working with. On a stable cotton fabric, a pencil or pen mark may work just fine, while other fabrics may respond poorly to that type of marking.

Various tools for marking:
- Pen and pencil
- Water-soluble marker
- Chalk
- Thread tacking (basting)
- Tracing wheel dressmaker's carbon paper
- Scissors
- Pins

→ *You will find the straight skirt on page 87, and the crewneck on page 55.*

Pressing

When we refer to pressing in the context of sewing, it simply means to iron, or more specifically to use the iron to press something in a certain direction. The iron is an invaluable companion when sewing, and we recommend always having it readily available near the sewing machine. Taking care to press all the seams as you work will result in a more professional and tidy finish. Be cautious with the temperature and use of steam on the iron, and use the correct setting for the fabric you are sewing with.

The sewing instructions indicate how to press seams, notches, and other details. As a rule, seam allowances should be pressed open when two pieces are sewn together. This involves folding the seam allowances to each side and pressing them outwards to lie flat.

Seam finishes

If you look on the inside of a garment you have bought, you will see that the seams are finished in a way that prevents the fabric from fraying and keeps the threads from unravelling. This serves both a practical and an aesthetic purpose. By securing the raw edges of the seams they become more durable, while also giving the garment a refined and more professional appearance.

There are various techniques for finishing seams. Some prefer to do this as preparation before assembling the garment, for example by sewing with overlock or zigzag stitch around all the cut edges. Alternatively you can finish the seams as you go, first sewing two pieces together and subsequently securing the edge by zigzagging or overlocking the seam allowances together after pressing the seam. Below we have listed some of the most commonly used methods for seam finishing.

Zigzag stitch
Most sewing machines have a zigzag stitch function as a standard setting. Choose the zigzag stitch on the sewing machine and sew along the edge. Try to get as close to the edge as possible to get a neat finish.

False overlock
Some sewing machines come with a special overlock seam (also called a false overlock). If your machine offers this feature, it typically includes a specialized presser foot that makes it easier to place the stitch along the fabric edge. What distinguishes this type of stitch from the zigzag stitch is that the stitch is wrapped around the edge.

Overlocker (serger)
For avid sewers, an overlocker machine can be a good investment. The overlocker features a built-in knife that trims the fabric edge as it operates. Simultaneously a straight stitch is sewn while loops of thread enclose the freshly-cut raw edge. This provides a clean and professional looking finish. An overlocker machine typically operates at a higher speed than a regular sewing machine.

Pinking shears
An easy way to finish the edges of delicate woven fabrics is to cut the edges with pinking shears, which create a zigzag edge. To some extent this prevents fraying but is not optimal for clothes that will be used and washed frequently.

French seam
A French seam provides an exclusive and neat finish to the seams and is performed as you sew the garment together. See page 170 for how to sew French seams.

Hong Kong finish
One of the most exquisite (and time-consuming) methods for seam finishing is perhaps the Hong Kong finish. Here, the seams are enclosed with bias binding, giving the garment an elevated and refined finish. Traditionally, the seam allowance is turned to the outside of the garment when using this method. It gives a unique look to the garment and is a challenge for those who want to take their sewing skills to the next level. See page 190 for how to sew bias binding.

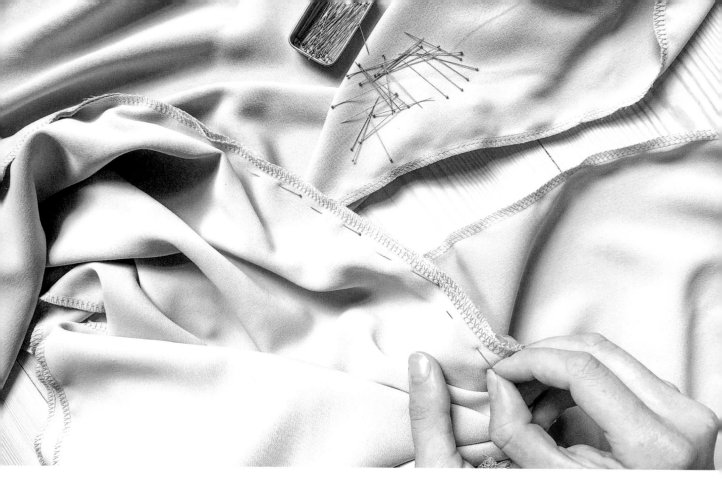

Using pins

Securing the pieces together with pins before stitching will make the sewing process easier and more precise. It ensures that the fabric is evenly distributed over the seam and prevents it from slipping and becoming crooked. The number of pins required varies depending on the type of fabric you are sewing with and the type of seam you are making. A curved seam (such as around the armhole) requires more pins than a straight seam, and a firm cotton fabric requires fewer pins than a smooth and thin fabric that slides easily.

- Place the pins so they can be removed easily as you sew, either with the head of the pin facing you, or placed crosswise so that you can grab the pin from the side.
- Place the pins along the seamline. This means that if you are using a 1 cm (⅜ in) seam allowance, the pins should be placed 1 cm (⅜ in) in from the edge of the fabric.
- Be careful to remove all the pins as you sew so that you do not sew over the pin and, in the worst case, end up breaking the needle.

← *You will find the wrap skirt on page 93, and the swimsuit on page 147.*

Tacking

A tacking (basting) stitch is a long stitch length used as a temporary stitch to hold pieces together. Sometimes using pins alone may not be sufficient to keep the pieces securely attached before sewing. In such cases it is better to use a tacking stitch to temporarily secure the pieces before proceeding with a regular seam. The tacking stitches are removed afterwards. Tacking can be sewn by machine or by hand.

Seam and stitch length

Vary the stitch length depending on the type of seams you are sewing. Seams that join two pieces and will not be visible from the outside should have a short stitch length to hold the garment together securely. A stitch length of 2.5, which is usually the standard setting for straight stitch on most sewing machines, is a good starting point for such seams. However, if you are working with thicker fabrics you might need to use a longer stitch length. When sewing visible stitches on the outside of the garment (topstitching), you should use a slightly longer stitch length of 3 to 3.5 for a neater appearance. Remember to secure the stitching at the beginning and end of each seam and cut off thread ends for each completed seam. This way, you avoid having to cut off all the thread ends when the garment is finished.

Interfacing

Fusible interfacing (or Vlieseline) is a fabric with adhesive on one side that can be ironed onto pieces of fabric to stabilize and reinforce them. It is commonly used on areas that require enhanced stability and reduced wrinkling, such as collars, waistbands and cuffs. Interfacing comes in different thicknesses, and it is advisable to choose interfacing that matches the fabric you are using. In other words, opt for thin interfacing for delicate fabrics and thicker interfacing for heavier materials. The pattern instructions will indicate when the use of interfacing is recommended.

Projects

The turtleneck, also known as a polo-neck or high-necked sweater, is a versatile and beloved garment that is a favourite of many. We consider it to be a go-to in most situations. Style it with jeans or a skirt, or layer it under a knit sweater – even a summer dress can be worn year-round with a comfortable turtleneck underneath. Our model can be varied with different neck heights and sleeve shapes, or it can be extended into a comfortable, high-necked dress.

Turtleneck sweater

You will need

Fabric
The table on page 223 shows the fabric requirement for the base pattern for a straight or fitted top in your size. It is important also to consider any adaptations, variations and parts you draw yourself when determining the final amount of fabric for your project.

Fabric suggestions
We recommend light to medium-weight jersey fabric with stretch. Choose a medium to heavy-weight knit for the dress.

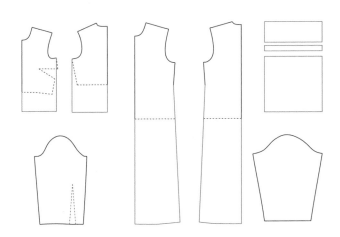

Pattern pieces

PATTERN PIECE	CUTTING INSTRUCTIONS	
	Sweater	*Dress*
Fitted top front piece ✎	Cut 1 on the fold	
Fitted top back piece ✎	Cut 1 on the fold	
Fitted sleeve	Cut 2	
Neck ✎	Cut 1	
Straight top front piece ✎		Cut 1
Straight top back piece ✎		Cut 1 on the fold
Straight sleeve		Cut 2

Pattern adjustments

Neck
The neck should be as wide as the circumference of the neckline of the top, plus 4 cm (1½ in) to allow for the shoulder seams, and you can choose the height of the neck. Here are some suggested measurements:
High neck with fold: Width x 40 cm (15¾ in) height
High neck without fold: Width x 15 cm (6 in) height
Low neck: Width x 4 cm (1½ in) height

Lengthening the sweater
The fitted sweater has a dart and finishes at the waist. To lengthen, remove the dart by extending the side seam with a vertical line from the top line of the dart to the desired length. Add about 30 cm (12 in) or take your body measurements to find the perfect length. Then extend the back piece with a vertical line to match the side seam of the adjusted front piece, from the tip of the armhole down.

→ *Long turtleneck dress with side split.*

Variations

Dress
To create a comfortable, high-necked dress in stretch fabric, use the pattern pieces for the straight top. Measure the desired length of the dress from the waist down and extend the pattern accordingly. Remember to add extra length for the hem at the bottom.

Slit
If you are making a long dress, add a slit in a side seam for better mobility. Finish the side seam above the bottom edge, press the seam allowance in the split to the wrong side and secure with a stitch from the right side.

Sleeves
The sweater is great with a straight sleeve, but you can vary them by making, for example, balloon sleeves with cuffs. See page 217 for how to create different sleeve shapes.

Before you begin:

Finish all raw edges by sewing a zigzag or overlock stitch around the pattern pieces. This step is not necessary if you plan to sew the sweater with an overlock machine (serger).

Sewing instructions

1.

Shoulder seams
Place the front and back pieces right sides together, and sew the shoulder seams. Press the seams open.

2.

Sleeves
Place the right side of one sleeve to the corresponding armhole, right sides together, and pin in place. Sew the sleeve into the armhole and press the seam. Repeat for the other sleeve.

On the fitted sleeve pattern there is a dart, but this dart should not be sewn when making the turtleneck sweater.

3.

Side seams
Place the front and back of the sweater together, right sides facing, aligning side and sleeve edges, and sew from the bottom of the sleeve, under the armhole, and down to the bottom of the sweater. Press the seams open. Repeat for the other side.

4.

Neck
Fold the neck piece right sides facing, aligning the short edges, and sew together. Then fold the neck lengthwise, wrong sides together, to hide the seam allowance on the inside of the neck, and press. Pin the neck to the neckline opening of the sweater, right sides together, and sew in place. To ensure that this seam is elastic, it is important to use a zigzag stitch or an overlock machine, if available.

5.

Hem
Fold the bottom edge of the sweater and both sleeves to make a 2 cm (¾ in) wide hem and topstitch in place.

We believe that every wardrobe should include a classic and feminine blouse that can be worn for many different occasions. A romantic blouse with balloon sleeves is a good starting point for any outfit. It can be combined with trousers (pants) and skirts. With its classic cut and voluminous sleeves with cuffs, our blouse includes all the elements essential for a long-lasting wardrobe favourite. Add features such as a large decorative collar or ruffle edges, which will make your blouse stand out from the crowd.

Blouse

You will need

Fabric
The table on page 223 shows the fabric requirement for the base pattern for a straight top in your size. It is important also to consider any adaptations, variations and parts you draw yourself when determining the final amount of fabric for your project. Remember to calculate extra fabric if you choose balloon sleeves.

Extras
- Fusible interfacing for facings and cuffs
- Invisible zip (35 cm/14 in) or hook-and-eye

Fabric suggestions
We recommend lightweight fabrics such as silk, chiffon, viscose, satin, lightweight cotton, or linen.

→ *Blouse with V-neck and decorative collar with ruffle edge combined with the straight skirt on page 87.*

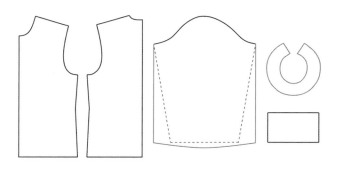

Pattern pieces

PATTERN PIECE	CUTTING INSTRUCTIONS
Straight top front piece	Cut 1 on the fold
Straight top back piece	Cut 2 – add seam allowance along the centre
Straight sleeve ✎	Cut 2
Cuff	Cut 2 + 2 in interfacing
Neckline facing ✎	Cut 1 on the fold + 1 on the fold in interfacing

Pattern adjustments

Facing
Draw a 6 cm (2⅜ in) wide facing for the neckline. See page 174 for how to draw a facing.

Balloon sleeves
Use the straight sleeve pattern to create a balloon sleeve with volume at the bottom. See page 217 for how to draw a facing.

Variations

Neckline
The blouse can be varied with different necklines. See page 220 for how to make different neckline shapes.

Closure
The blouse features a back closure: choose whether to insert an invisible zip or make a slit opening with a hook. If you make a neckline large enough to fit your head, you can cut the back piece on the fold and omit the closure.

Decorative collar
The blouse gets a little extra flair with a large collar. See page 208 for how to design your own decorative collar.

Iron interfacing onto the cuffs, facings and collar. Finish all raw edges by sewing a zigzag or overlock stitch around the pattern pieces.

Sewing instructions

1.

Closure

For an invisible zip closure   Insert the zip between the two back pieces on the centre back seam. The teeth of the zip should start 1 cm (⅜ in) from the neck opening to allow for the facing. See page 178 for how to insert an invisible zip. Complete the centre back seam from the lower edge to the zip, and press open.

For a slit closure   Place the back pieces right sides together. Measure 20 cm (8 in) from the neckline down along the centre back seam and make a mark for the bottom of the slit. Sew the centre back seam from the lower edge to the mark. Press the seam open and the seam allowance on the slit towards the wrong side.

2.

Shoulder seams
Place the front and back pieces right sides together, and sew the shoulder seams. Press the seams open.

3.

Decorative collar (optional)
See page 208 for how to sew a decorative collar.

4.

Facing
Attach the facing, right sides together, to the neckline and sew in place. If you have included a decorative collar, place it between the facing and the neck opening. See page 174 for how to sew a facing with or without an invisible zip.

For a slit closure   Topstitch along the edges of the slit to secure the seam allowance. Sew a hook-and-eye at the top of the neck opening by hand.

5.

Sleeves
Fold the cuff lengthwise, wrong sides together, and press. Open out the cuff again and press one long edge 1 cm (⅜ in) towards the wrong side.

6.

Sew a gathering stitch on the lower edge of both sleeves and gather the fabric to fit the cuff. See page 184 for how to gather. Sew the bottom edge of the sleeve to the unfolded edge of the cuff, right sides together. Press the seam allowance towards the sleeve. Repeat on the other sleeve.

7. With the blouse right side facing you, pin one sleeve right sides together to the corresponding armhole. Sew in place and press the seam open. Repeat for the other sleeve.

8. **Side seams**
With the blouse right sides together, sew from the bottom of the cuff, under the armhole, and to the bottom of the blouse. Press the seam open. Repeat on the other side.

9. Fold the cuff over to the wrong side and sew the folded edge to the seam allowance between the sleeve and the cuff. Remove the gathering stitches.

10. **Hem**
Fold up and press the bottom edge of the blouse by 1 cm (⅜ in) towards the wrong side twice, so that the raw edge is hidden inside the fold. Topstitch from the right side to secure the hem.

Tip! *Shirring can be a great feature on this blouse. For example, you can sew a few rounds of shirring along the bottom edge or replace the cuff with shirring at the bottom of the sleeves. If you want to use shirring on the sleeve, we recommend extending the sleeve pattern by 10 cm (4 in) before cutting the fabric. See page 192 for how to shirr fabric.*

The classic shirt featuring a button stand (placket), collar and cuffs is an essential wardrobe staple. It's easily recognizable with distinctive design elements but can vary greatly when it comes to cutting and construction. The shirt is often associated with tailoring, but you don't have to be a tailor to make one. Our model is simple with a straight cut that is both attractive and comfortable to wear. With fabrics such as linen, cotton and silk, you can create a flattering shirt to be enjoyed for a long time.

Shirt

You will need

Fabric
The table on page 223 shows the fabric requirements for the base pattern for a straight top in your size. It is important also to consider any adaptations, variations and parts you draw yourself when determining the final amount of fabric for your project.

Extras
- Interfacing for collar and cuffs
- 8–10 buttons

Fabric suggestions
We recommend lightweight woven cotton for a timeless look. Choose linen or silk for a touch of elegance.

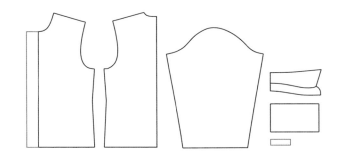

← *Shirt combined with trousers on page 101, and the baguette bag on page 153.*

Pattern pieces

PATTERN PIECE	CUTTING INSTRUCTIONS
Straight top front piece ✎	Cut 2
Straight top back piece	Cut 1 on the fold
Straight sleeve	Cut 2
Cuff	Cut 2 + 2 in interfacing
Shirt collar	Cut 2 on the fold + 2 on the fold in interfacing
Sleeve placket ✎	Cut 2

Pattern adjustments

Front panel with button stand (placket)
To incorporate the button stand, extend the width of the front panel in the centre front by 6 cm (2⅜ in). Extend the point at the centre of the neckline 6 cm (2⅜ in) outwards and do the same for the bottom edge of the shirt. Draw a vertical line between the points where you have extended.

Sleeve placket
The measurement for the sleeve placket piece is 3 x 20 cm (1¼ x 8 in).

Before you begin

Iron interfacing onto the collar and cuffs. Finish all raw edges by sewing a zigzag or overlock stitch around the pattern pieces. It is not necessary to finish the raw edges of the collar and button stand (placket).

Sewing instructions

1.

Sleeves
Sew the pleats at the bottom of each sleeve according to the markings on the pattern. Press the pleats in place. See page 186 for how to sew pleats.

2.

Sleeve placket
Cut open along the marking at the end of the sleeve to make a T-shape slit. Repeat for the other sleeve.

Press one long side of the placket piece by 0.5 cm (¼ in) towards the wrong side.

3.

From the wrong side, open the slit so that it lies in a straight line and attach the unpressed long side of the placket piece. Sew about 0.5 cm (¼ in) from the edge, making sure to catch the T-shape cuts within the seam allowance.

Fold the placket over towards the right side of the sleeve and pin in place, slightly covering the stitch line. Sew in place close to the folded edge and press.

Fold the sleeve right sides together along the slit. Sew diagonally across the fold line at the top of the slit. Begin the stitching right at the existing stitch line, stitching only over the placket to avoid bulk. Stop 1–2 mm (1/16 in) short of the stitching line. See the picture on page 53.

Repeat steps 2 and 3 for the other sleeve.

4.

Button stand
Press the centre front raw edge on the left front piece by 1 cm (⅜ in) towards the wrong side. Press again by 2.5 cm (1 in) encasing the raw edge in the fold. Topstitch the button stand from the right side. Make sure to catch the folded edge on the wrong side in the stitching. Repeat for the other front piece.

5.

Shoulder seams
Place the front pieces right sides together on the back piece and sew the shoulder seams. Press both the seams open.

6.

Shirt collar

Place the collar pieces with right sides facing and sew them together along all the outer edges, except for the bottom curve (the edge that will be sewn to the neckline). Trim the corners and make small cuts in the seam allowance on the tightest curves. Turn the collar right side out and press. Use a knitting needle to gently push out the points from the wrong side.

Fold and press the bottom edge of one of the collar pieces 1 cm (⅜ in) towards the wrong side.

Place the unpressed edge towards the wrong side of the neckline and sew in place. Fold and pin the collar to the right side of the shirt. The folded edge will enclose the seam allowance inside the collar. Topstitch from the right side along the fold edge. Topstitch around the outer edges of the collar with a 0.5 cm (¼ in) seam allowance.

Fold down the collar, creating an integrated collar stand. Press and shape the collar as desired.

7.

Sleeves

With the shirt right side facing you, pin one sleeve right sides together to the corresponding armhole. Sew and press the seam open. Repeat for the other sleeve.

8.

Side seams

With the shirt right sides together, align the side and sleeve edges and sew from the bottom of the sleeve, under the armhole, and down to the hem. Press the seam open. Repeat on the other side.

9.

Cuffs

Fold one cuff in half lengthwise, right sides together, and sew the short sides together. Clip the corners, turn right side out, and press. Press one long side of the cuff 1 cm (⅜ in) towards the wrong side.

Place the unfolded long side of the cuff right sides together against the wrong side of the sleeve and sew in place. Fold the cuff to the right side and pin in place along the right side of the sleeve, so the folded edge hides the seam allowance inside the cuff. Topstitch from the right side along the folded edge.

Complete the cuff by topstitching along the other three sides, about 0.5 cm (¼ in) from the edge.

Repeat for the other cuff.

10.

Hem

Fold the bottom edge of the shirt 1 cm (⅜ in) towards the wrong side and press. Fold it over again and press, so the seam allowance is hidden inside the hem. Sew it in place with a stitch from the right side.

11.

Buttons and buttonholes

Sew buttonholes on the cuffs and button stand (placket) with a sewing machine. We recommend 6–8 buttons evenly spaced along the button stand and 1 button for each cuff.

Use the buttonholes as a guide to ensure that the buttons are sewn in the right place. We recommend buttoning each button as it is sewn to ensure that the spacing is even down the button stand.

See page 172 for further instructions on buttons and buttonholes.

The crewneck, college sweater, sweatshirt, or pullover is adored by fashion-lovers all over the world, as it is the essence of 'casual cool'. The sweater has its origins in the world of sports, and was used by rowers, and other athletes. Today, it is a key item in most wardrobes – it is hard to resist a soft and comfortable crewneck, which can be combined with almost anything. In vibrant colours, it makes you shine, even on days when you don't feel like putting in a lot of effort into your outfit. Carry it with you in your bag, so you are always prepared to layer up when a chill sets in.

Crewneck

You will need

Fabric
The table on page 223 shows the fabric requirements for the base pattern for a straight top in your size. It is important also to consider any adaptations, variations and parts you draw yourself when determining the final amount of fabric for your project.

Extras
◦ Ribbing fabric (30 cm/12 in)

Fabric suggestions
We recommend classic sweatshirt fabrics such as French terry or fleece for this project.

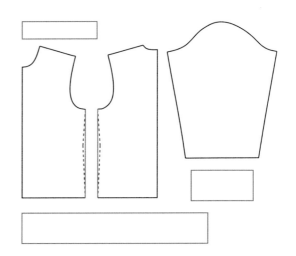

Pattern pieces

We recommend going up one size for a more oversized fit.

PATTERN PIECE	CUTTING INSTRUCTIONS
Straight top front piece ✐	Cut 1 on the fold
Straight top back piece ✐	Cut 1 on the fold
Straight sleeve	Cut 2
Ribbed neckline ✐	Cut 1
Ribbed cuff ✐	Cut 2
Ribbed hem ✐	Cut 1

Pattern adjustments

Ribbing
Calculate the width of the ribbed edges by multiplying
the measurement of where you will sew the ribbing by 0.8 for the neckline
and body and 0.6 for the sleeve and you can choose the ribbing depth.
Here are some suggested measurements to draw each piece:
Neckline: Width x 8 cm (3⅛ in) depth
Hem: Width x 14 cm (5½ in) depth
Cuff: Width x 14 cm (5½ in) depth

Fit and length
Decrease the length of both front and back pattern pieces by 8 cm (3⅛ in).
Also, rather than following the waist indentation on the pattern, cut a straight
line from the bottom of the armhole to the hemline to create a straight
silhouette for the top.

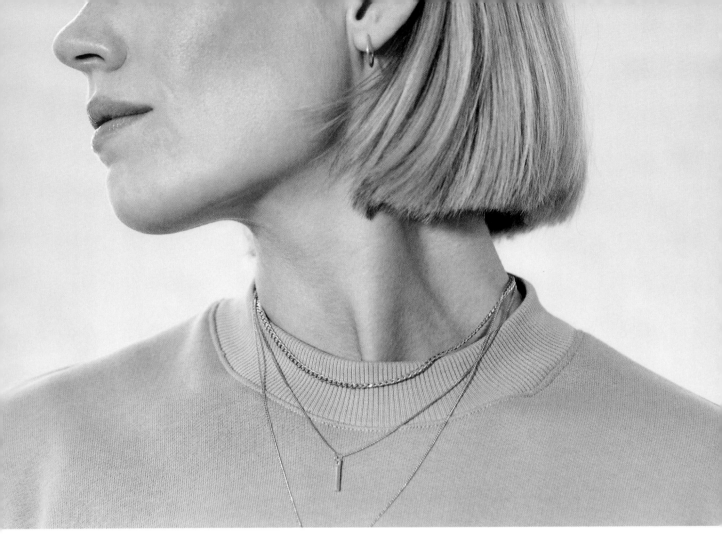

Variations

Colourblocking can give the sweater some extra flair. To create this effect, divide the pattern pieces into smaller sections and cut them out separately in fabrics of different colours or patterns. Remember to add seam allowances along the cut edges.

It is also possible to create a colourblock effect without dividing the pattern pieces by using fabric in different colours on the original pieces, such as a contrasting colour on the sleeves or ribbed edges.

Before you begin

Finish all raw edges by sewing a zigzag or overlock stitch around the pattern pieces. This step is not necessary if you plan to sew the sweater using an overlock machine (serger).

Sewing instructions

1.

Shoulder seams
Place the front and back pieces right sides together, and sew the shoulder seams. Press the seams open.

2.

Sleeves
Place the top with the right side facing up and pin one sleeve, right sides together, to the corresponding armhole. Sew and press the seam open. Repeat for the other sleeve.

3.

Side seams
Place the sweater right sides together, aligning side and sleeve edges, and sew from the bottom of the sleeve, under the armhole, and down to the bottom edge of the sweater. Press the seam open. Repeat for the other side.

4.

Ribbing
Fold the neckline ribbing in half right sides together, and sew the short edges together, forming a circle. Press the seam open. Then fold the ribbing circle lengthwise with the wrong side facing (the seam allowance is now hidden on the inside) and press.

5.

Attach the ribbing, right sides together, to the neckline of the sweater. Since the ribbing is shorter than the circumference of the neckline, it must be stretched and pinned in place before sewing. To make this seam elastic, sew with a zigzag stitch or an overlock machine.

Topstitch from the right side around the opening after the ribbing is attached to keep the seam allowance in place on the wrong side.

6.

Repeat steps 4 and 5 to add the cuff ribbing to both the sleeves.

7.

Repeat steps 4 and 5 to add the hem ribbing to the bottom hemline.

Tip! *How about decorating the sweater with iron-on patches or embroidering a small design?*

In our quest for the perfect T-shirt, we have come to realize that finding the definitive answer is not easy. Even though it is a simple garment, small details can make a significant difference in whether a T-shirt becomes a beloved everyday piece – or remains tucked away in the wardrobe. Rather then presenting you with a predetermined formula, we want to give you the best foundation possible to create your own perfect T-shirt, with the details you like best. Whether you prefer an oversized or slim fit, with long, short, or no sleeves, or with a round or V-neck – just decide what you like and create your perfect combination.

T-shirt

You will need

Fabric
The table on page 223 shows the fabric requirements for the base pattern for a straight or fitted top in your size. It is important also to consider any adaptations, variations and parts you draw yourself when determining the final amount of fabric for your project.

Extras
- Ribbing (10 cm/4 in)

Fabric suggestions
We recommend using light- to medium-weight jersey fabric with some stretch.

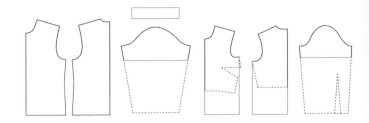

Pattern pieces

Consider going up or down in size based on how you prefer the fit. See variations for more information.

PATTERN PIECE	CUTTING INSTRUCTIONS	
	Oversized	*Fitted*
Straight top front piece	Cut 1 on the fold	
Straight top back piece	Cut 1 on the fold	
Straight sleeve ✎	Cut 2	
Fitted top front piece ✎		Cut 1 on the fold
Fitted top back piece ✎		Cut 1 on the fold
Fitted sleeve ✎		Cut 2
Ribbed neckline ✎	Cut 1	Cut 1

Measuring

Lengthening front and back pieces (for fitted style only):
The fitted top has a dart and finishes at the waist. To lengthen, remove the dart by extending the side seam with a vertical line from the top line of the dart to the desired length. Add about 35 cm (14 in) or take your body measurements to find the perfect length. Then extend the back piece with a vertical line to match the side seam of the adjusted front piece, from the tip of the armhole down.

Ribbing
Calculate the width of the ribbing by multiplying the circumference of the neckline by 0.8. Here is a suggested measurement to draw the pattern:
Neckline: Width x 8 cm (3⅛ in) depth

Sleeves
Choose the length of the sleeve based on your preference, but keep the shape of the sleeve cap intact. Mark the desired length on the pattern and remember to add 2 cm (¾ in) for the hem.

→ *Fitted T-shirt.*

Variations

Neckline
T-shirts usually have a round or V-shape neckline. The base patterns have a round neckline, but you can make the opening larger. See page 220 for how to change the neckline.

Fit
Oversized or fitted? The main difference between using the straight or fitted top pattern pieces lies in the shoulder seam and sleeves. The straight top has a wide shoulder and wider sleeves; the fitted top is more tailored.
For a tighter fit, go down one or more sizes. For an extra wide fit, go up one or more sizes.

63

Finish all raw edges by sewing a zigzag or overlock stitch around the pattern pieces. This step is not necessary if you plan to sew the T-shirt with an overlock machine (serger).

Sewing instructions

1.

Shoulder seams
Place the front and back pieces right sides together, and sew the shoulder seams. Press the seams open.

2.

Sleeves
Place the top with the right side facing up and pin one sleeve, right sides together, to the corresponding armhole. Sew together and press the seam open. Repeat for the other sleeve.

3.

Side seams
Place the T-shirt right sides together, aligning side and sleeve edges, and sew from the bottom of the sleeve, under the armhole, and down to the bottom edge of the shirt. Repeat for the other side.

4.

Ribbing
For a round neckline   Fold the ribbing right sides together, and sew the short ends to form a circle. Fold the ribbing circle lengthwise wrong sides facing (the seam allowance is hidden on the inside), and press.

For a V-neckline   Fold the ribbing in half, wrong side out, and lay it along one side of the neckline so the bottom corner of the ribbing is aligned with the bottom point of the neckline. Imagine a straight line up from the bottom point of the V and cut the ribbing at a diagonal along this line. Use the cut off piece as a template to cut the other short end of the ribbing. Place the ribbing right sides together to sew a seam along the diagonal edge. When you fold the ribbing double, with the right side out, it will form a V-neck shape.

5.

Attach the ribbing to the neckline of the shirt right sides together. Since the ribbing is shorter than the circumference of the neckline, stretch and pin it before sewing in place. To make this seam elastic, sew with a zigzag stitch or an overlock machine.

6.

Hem
Fold the bottom edge of the T-shirt and both sleeves up with a 2 cm (¾ in) wide hem and topstitch in place.

←   *Oversized T-shirt combined with wrap skirt on page 93.*

Flipping through a fashion magazine without spotting at least one street-style influencer sporting an oversized blazer is nearly impossible. Blazers have become a staple in the Norwegian fashion scene and for good reason. Once considered a symbol of men's fashion, women have embraced blazers for decades, starting as early as the 1940s when blazers became a symbol of women's fight for equality. The popularity skyrocketed in the 1980s with the emergence of power suits featuring bold shoulder pads, large buttons, and vibrant designs. Our version of the blazer features a straight cut and lining. You can customize it with shoulder pads or pockets to suit your style. Drape it elegantly over your shoulders at a summer party, or make it your go-to everyday jacket. This one is guaranteed to become a favourite!

Blazer

You will need

Fabric
The table on page 223 shows the fabric requirements for the base pattern for a jacket in your size.
It is important also to consider any adaptations, variations and parts you draw yourself when determining the final amount of fabric needed for your project.

Extras
- Interfacing for the collar
- 2 buttons
- Shoulder pads – optional
- Lining fabric

Fabric suggestions
We recommend choosing a light- to medium-weight wool with a smooth surface. For the lining, slippery satin is a good option.

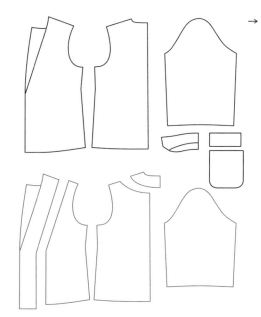

→ *Blazer combined with turtleneck sweater on page 35.*

Pattern pieces

PATTERN PIECE	CUTTING INSTRUCTIONS
Jacket front piece	Cut 2
Jacket back piece	Cut 2
Jacket sleeves	Cut 2
Jacket collar	Cut 2 on the fold + 2 on the fold in interfacing
Lining front piece ✎	Cut 2
Lining back piece ✎	Cut 2
Lining sleeve ✎	Cut 2
Neckline facing ✎	Cut 2
Front piece facing ✎	Cut 2

Pattern adjustments

Facing
Draw a facing 10 cm (4 in) wide for the neckline and front opening. For the front piece, measure 10 cm (4 in) from the dotted line marking the lapel fold; the facing covers the lapel + 10 cm (4 in). See illustration above and page 174.

Lining
To create the lining pattern pieces, copy the front and back but 3 cm (1¼ in) shorter and minus the interfacing. Remember to add 1 cm (⅜ in) seam allowance along the edge between the lining and interfacing – or draw the pieces without this seam allowance, but add it when cutting. The sleeve lining fabric is 7 cm (2¾ in) shorter than the sleeves in the outer fabric.

68

Variations

Pockets

For a contemporary style, sew large patch pockets on the front of the blazer. Choose welt pockets with flaps for a clean look. You can also combine the latter with a breast pocket for a classic blazer look. See pages 200–207 for how to sew different pockets. Remember to sew on any pockets before sewing the lining into the blazer.

Shoulder pads

Shoulder pads can enhance the silhouette of the blazer providing structure and shape. When selecting shoulder pads, choose a triangular shape that builds up the shoulder area. The size depends on the thickness of the fabric. Lighter fabrics may require less volume, while heavier fabrics may benefit from pads with more volume to define the shape. Remember to sew the shoulder pads in place before sewing the lining onto the blazer.

Iron interfacing onto the collar and, if applicable, the pocket flap. Finish all raw edges by sewing zigzag or overlock stitches around the pattern pieces.

Sewing instructions

1.

Centre back seam
Place the back pieces in the outer fabric right sides together, and sew the centre back seam. Press the seam open.

2.

Shoulder seams
With the front pieces and back piece right sides together, align and then sew the shoulder seams. Press the seams open.

3.

Side seams
With the front pieces right sides facing the back piece, align the side seams and sew together, starting from the armhole down to the hem. Press the seam open.

4.

Sleeves
Fold one sleeve lengthwise, right sides together and aligning edges, and sew the seam. Press the seam open. Repeat for the other sleeve.

5.

Turn the blazer inside out and insert the sleeves into the armholes from the inside, right sides together. Pin and sew around the armholes to attach the sleeve.

6.

Press the hemline of the sleeve and blazer 4 cm (1½ in) towards the wrong side.

7.

Facing
Place the neckline pieces right sides together. Align the centre back edges and sew together. Place the shoulder edges of the front facing right sides together with the shoulder edges of the neckline facing. Sew together, so they become one long piece. Press the seams open.

8.

Lining
Sew the lining pieces together the same way as you did for the outer fabric in steps 1–5.

9.

Mark a notch 3 cm (1¼ in) above the hemline on both front pieces of the lining.

10. Align the facing with the outer edge of the lining, right sides together. Match the centre back seam and the shoulder seams. The facing will extend 3 cm (1¼ in) beyond the lining hemline on each side. Sew and then press the seam allowance towards the facing.

11. Collar
Place the collar pieces right sides together, and sew from notch to notch. Trim the corners and clip the seam allowance, then turn inside out, using a knitting needle to gently push out the corners, and press.

12. Place the collar onto the neckline of the blazer, right sides together. Align the centre of the collar with the centre back of the blazer and match the notches on the lapel. Sew the collar to the neckline with a 0.5 cm (¼ in) seam allowance.

13. Shoulder pads and pockets (optional):
If you want to insert shoulder pads or pockets in the blazer, you must do this before sewing the outer fabric together with the lining and facing.

14. Now you will attach the lining and facing to the blazer. Turn the blazer lining wrong side out. The blazer in the outer fabric should be right side out. Place the blazer in the outer fabric inside the lining fabric, right sides together. Align the outer edges and pin around the opening of the blazer.

15. Start at the bottom by sewing a horizontal seam across the facing following the fold you pressed in step 6, 4 cm (1½ in) up from the bottom edge. Next stitch along the outer edge, starting from the hemline and working up to connect the lining to the blazer. Make sure the collar is inside the two fabrics when sewing over the neckline. Finish by sewing a horizontal seam across the facing on the opposite side.

16. Clip the seam allowance along the curved neck edge to create a smooth curve, and trim the corner on the lapel. Trim the excess fabric at the bottom to avoid bulk in the lower corner when turning right side out.

17. Turn the blazer right side out, with the lining on the inside. Press the collar and front edge well. You can also topstitch along the edge to maintain the shape of the lapel and collar.

→   *Blazer combined with turtleneck on page 35, and trousers on page 101.*

18.

Lining the sleeves

Insert your hand between the lining and outer fabric and turn one sleeve in the outer fabric wrong side out between the layers. Retrieve the corresponding sleeve in the lining fabric, so that this sleeve is also wrong side out. Join these sleeves by unfolding the cut end on the sleeve and pinning to the end of the lining, right sides together, to form one long tube. Sew together.

Pull the sleeve through the armhole from the right side of the blazer. The sleeve will now fold along the crease made in step 6 with the lining on the inside. Repeat for the other sleeve.

19.

Hem

Fold the hem of the blazer up along the edge that you pressed in step 6. Slip stitch the folded edge down all around. See page 166 for how to slip stitch.

Press the hemline of the lining up by 1 cm (⅜ in) and then up again by 1.5 cm (⅝ in), enclosing the raw edge in the fold. Topstitch around the hem on the lining.

Connect the gap between the lining and the facing on each side with a couple of slip stitches. The lining will now neatly cover the blazer hem.

20.

Buttons and buttonholes

Hand or machine sew buttonholes on the right front piece as marked on the pattern. The blazer only requires two buttons, so use the top two markings. Sew buttons on the left front as marked on the pattern sheet.

Tip! *You can buy buttons that you can cover yourself. It can be an extra stylish detail with buttons covered in the same fabric as the blazer.*

On blustery winter days, nothing is quite so delightful as slipping into a warm and snug wool coat. With our ever-changing climate and frigid temperatures, we firmly believe that a coat is indispensable in any wardrobe. Our coat boasts a straight, slightly oversized design, striking the perfect balance between practicality and elegance. To accentuate the silhouette, we have incorporated a tie belt at the waist. All seam edges on the inside are concealed with bias binding, known as a 'Hong Kong finish', giving the garment an extra touch of exclusivity.

Coat

You will need

Fabric
The table on page 223 shows the fabric requirements for the base pattern for a jacket in your size. It is important also to consider any adaptations, variations, and parts you draw yourself when determining the final amount of fabric for your project. Remember to calculate extra fabric to extend the length of the coat pattern.

Extras
- Bias binding for seam edges (15–20 m/16½–22 yd)
- Fusible interfacing for collar and pocket flap
- 3 buttons

Fabric suggestions
We recommend using a mid- to heavy-weight wool for a durable autumn and winter coat. Lighter options, such as cotton twill or gaberdine will make it suitable for springtime.

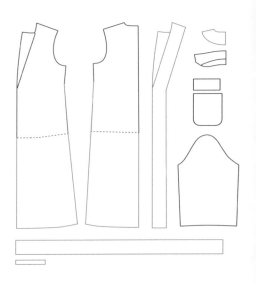

Pattern pieces

PATTERN PIECE	CUTTING INSTRUCTIONS
Jacket front piece ✏	Cut 2
Jacket back piece ✏	Cut 2
Jacket sleeves	Cut 2
Jacket collar	Cut 2 on the fold + 2 on the fold in interfacing
Jacket pocket flap	Cut 2 + 2 in interfacing
Jacket pocket bag	Cut 2 long + 2 short (dotted line)
Neckline facing ✏	Cut 2
Front piece facing ✏	Cut 2
Tie belt ✏	Cut 1

Variations

Length
The coat should be calf-length. To adjust the length, measure the distance from the waist down to your preferred length. Remember to add 4 cm/1½ in for the hem at the bottom.

Pattern adjustments

Lengthen the coat and vent
Extend the centre line on the front piece from the waist on the pattern down to your preferred length. Remember to add 4 cm (1½ in) for the hem at the bottom. Draw a horizontal line from the bottom point at a right angle for the bottom edge. Extend the side seam by continuing the line until it meets the bottom line. Mark a point on the side 3 cm (1¼ in) above the bottom line. Draw a line from this mark, curving it slightly to intersect the bottom line, for the new hemline. Repeat for the back piece, ensure the side edges match.

Add a vent extension to the back piece. Start by extending the bottom line at the centre back with a horizontal line measuring 6 cm (2⅜ in). From this point, draw a vertical line straight up measuring 45 cm (17¾ in). Then draw a diagonal line that intersects the centre back line 5 cm (2 in) above.

Facing
Draw a 10 cm (4 in) wide facing for the neckline and front opening of the coat. On the front piece, measure 10 cm (4 in) from the line that marks the fold line for the lapel, the facing should cover the lapel plus 10 cm (4 in). See the illustration on the previous page and page 174 for more information on facings.

Tie belt and belt loops
See page 210 for how to make a tie belt and belt loops for the waist. You only need two belt loops, one in each side seam. You can also choose to use a belt with a buckle instead of tie bands.

Iron interfacing onto the collar and pocket flap. The coat will be finished with bias binding around the raw edges on the inside, also known as a 'Hong Kong finish'. See page 190 for how to sew bias binding.

Sewing instructions

1.

Tie belt and belt loops
Sew tie belt and belt loops following the instructions on page 210.

2.

Facing
Place the neckline pieces right sides together. Align the centre back edges and sew together. Place the shoulder edges of the front facing right sides together with the shoulder edges of the neckline facing. Sew together, so they become one long piece. Press the seams open.

3.

Attach bias binding along the inner raw edge of the facing – this is the edge not shaped to the lapel. Finish the opposite edge with zigzag or overlock stitch.

4.

Attach bias binding along the centre edge of both back pieces, following the contour of the vent extension you drew when you extended the coat.

5.

Vent
See page 194 for how to sew a vent.

6.

Pockets
Sew single welt pockets to the pocket markings on the front piece. See page 204 for instructions. Sew bias binding along the edges of the pocket bags after you have sewn the pocket pieces together.

7.

Shoulder seams
Attach bias binding along the shoulder edges on the back piece and front pieces.

→ *Coat combined with turtleneck on page 35.*

8. With the front pieces and back piece right sides together, sew the shoulder seams and press open.

9. **Side seams**
Pin a belt loop at the waistline in each side seam, aligning the raw edges of the loop with the side edge.

Attach bias binding along the side edges of the front and back pieces, leaving the armhole edge raw. Finish the centre front edge with a zigzag or overlock stitch.

10. Place the front pieces onto the back piece, right sides together. Align the side edges and sew the side seam, ensuring the belt loops are sandwiched between the back and front pieces. Press the seams open.

11. Attach bias binding along the hemline of the coat.

12. **Sleeves**
Attach bias binding along the sides and bottom edge of both sleeves, leaving the top edge raw.

13. Press the bottom edge of the sleeve 4 cm (1½ in) towards the wrong side to create a crease. Then fold the sleeve lengthwise, right sides together and aligning the edges, and sew down the centre of the sleeve. Press the seam open. Repeat for the other sleeve.

14. Fold up the hemline on the crease you made previously and slip stitch by hand or blind stitch on the sewing machine. See page 166 for how to slip stitch.

15. Turn the coat inside out and insert the sleeve into the armhole from the inside, right sides together. Pin and sew around the armhole. Repeat for the other sleeve. Attach bias binding around the armhole of both sleeves.

16. **Collar**
Place the collar pieces right sides together, and sew from notch to notch. Trim the corners and clip the seam allowance, then turn inside out, using a knitting needle to gently push out the corners, and press.

17. Place the collar on the neckline, right sides together, aligning the centre of the collar with the centre back seam of the coat and matching the notches with the lapel. Sew the collar to the neckline with a 0.5 cm (¼ in) seam allowance.

18. Facing
Place the facing right sides together with the front opening of the coat. Align the outer edges and pin to hold them together. Start at the bottom by sewing a horizontal seam 4 cm (1½ in) up from the bottom edge. Then sew along the outer edge, starting from the hemline and moving up. Make sure the collar is sandwiched between the two pieces as you sew the neckline. Finish with a seam 4 cm (1½ in) up from the bottom edge across the hem on the opposite side.

19. Clip the seam allowance around the curved neckline and trim off the corner of the lapel. Trim the excess fabric of the facing to reduce bulk when you turn the coat right side out.

20. Turn the coat right side out. Press the collar and the front edge well. You can also topstitch along the edge to maintain the shape of the collar and lapel.

21. Hem
Press the hemline up by 4 cm (1½ in) all around. Hem by hand with a slip stitch or use a blind stitch on the sewing machine around the entire edge. See page 166 for how to slip stitch.

22. Buttons and buttonholes
Hand or machine sew buttonholes on the right front piece as marked on the pattern. Sew buttons onto the left front piece as marked on the pattern.

Tip! *You can buy buttons that you can cover with fabric yourself. It can be an extra stylish detail to use fabric that matches the coat for the buttons.*

A classic, straight skirt is a feminine garment that belongs in every wardrobe. With the right styling, this type of skirt effortlessly transitions from Sunday dinner with your grandmother to a night out on the town. Our model is a good starting point for unleashing your creativity – the skirt can easily be varied with different lengths, fabrics, colours and stitching details. So, whether you prefer a classic pencil skirt or a thigh-high mini skirt, you should be able to create a garment that reflects your style.

Straight skirt

You will need

Fabric
The table on page 223 shows the fabric requirements for the base pattern for a skirt in your size. It is important also to consider any adaptations, variations and parts you draw yourself when determining the final amount of fabric needed for your project.

Extras
- Interfacing for waistband and for fly facing (optional)
- Button
- Invisible zip for side closure (30 cm/12 in) or regular zip for fly front zip (20 cm/8 in)

Fabric suggestions
Lightweight fabrics such as linen, satin or crepe fabric offer a breezy and summery look, while heavier fabrics such as wool, denim or faux leather give a more structured appearance that is suitable for cooler seasons.

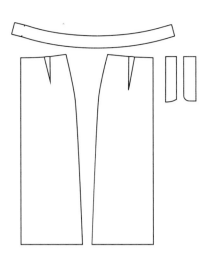

← *Straight skirt with closing on the side.*

Pattern pieces

PATTERN PIECES	CUTTING INSTRUCTIONS	
	Side closure	*Fly closure*
Skirt front piece	Cut 1 on the fold	Cut 2 – add seam allowance along the centre line
Skirt back piece	Cut 1 on the fold	Cut 1 on the fold
Waistband	Cut 2 + 2 in interfacing	Cut 2 + 2 in interfacing
Fly facing		Cut 1 + 1 in interfacing
Fly flap		Cut 1 on the fold

Variations

Length
The pattern pieces are marked mini and midi length, but you can measure from the waist to your desired length, adding 4 cm (1½ in) extra for the hem.

Slit
You can add a slit on the sides, front or back. For a slit in the middle of the front or back, the front or back pieces must be cut in two parts instead of on a fold, allowing for a centre seam. Remember to add 1 cm (⅜ in) seam allowance along the original fold edge.

Closure
The skirt can be closed with a hidden zip on the side or with a fly front zip. The latter option is a cool detail in thicker fabrics like denim or canvas.
If you want to sew a fly front zip the front piece must be cut into two parts.

Pockets
Pockets are both practical and can be a stylish detail. See pages 200–202 for how to sew pockets in-seam or on the skirt front.

89

Iron the interfacing onto the waistband pieces and onto the optional fly facing. Finish all raw edges by zigzag stitching or overlocking around the pattern pieces.

Sewing instructions

1.

Darts
Sew the darts on the front and back pieces according to the pattern markings. See page 184 for how to sew darts.

2.

Closure
For a side closure   Sew the zip in place, right sides together, on the left front piece. The teeth of the zip should be placed 1 cm (⅜ in) from the top. The other side of the zip is sewn in place on the left back piece in the same way. See page 178 for how to sew an invisible zip.

For a closure with a fly   Sew the fly at the top between the two front pieces as explained on page 180.

3.

Side seams
Place the front and back pieces right sides together, and sew the side seams. If you have chosen an invisible zip, sew up to the bottom of the zip on the side with the zip. For a closure with a fly, the side seams should be sewn in their entirety. Press the seams open.

4.

Waistband
Place the two waistband pieces right sides together, and sew along the short sides and top edge. Clip the corners and along the curve if necessary. Turn the waistband right side out and press.

5.

Press the seam allowance along one long side of the waistband 1 cm (⅜ in) towards the wrong side. This will be the front of the waistband.

6.

Place the back of the waistband with the right side facing the wrong side of the skirt.

For a side closure   Pin the waistband to the top edge of the skirt, starting from the zip on the front piece. The waistband should extend about 4 cm (1½ in) beyond the zip on the back piece.

For a closure with a fly   Pin the waistband to the top edge of the skirt, from the fly flap around to the opposite side.

Sew the waistband in place and press the seam allowance up towards the waistband.

↑ *Straight skirt with patch pockets on page 202.*

7.

Turn the waistband over to the right side and press. Topstitch along the folded edge of the waistband from the right side.

For a side closure As you reach the extension on the back piece, fold the bottom edge by 1 cm (⅜ in) towards the wrong side to conceal the raw edge. Align the ends of the waistband and continue topstitching align the folded edge.

8.

Hem
Fold the hemline up by 1 cm (⅜ in) and then by 3 cm (1¼ in) and slip stitch in place. See page 166 for how to slip stitch.

9.

Buttonhole and buttons
Sew buttonholes with a sewing machine. With a side closure, the buttonhole is placed on the waistband above the zip on the front piece. The waistband extension on the back piece is placed under the buttonhole for the button.

The wrap skirt is undoubtedly a wardrobe winner! Its tie waist gives a flattering appearance, while the wrap style ensures a comfortable fit. Play around with different lengths or detailing to create different looks. Add a ruffled hem to a long skirt for a dreamy romantic look, or cut a short skirt with clean lines for a sleeker style. Combine the skirt with a T-shirt and sneakers for a casual outfit on hot summer days, or with a turtleneck, tights and boots when the leaves start to fall from the trees.

Wrap skirt

You will need

Fabric
The table on page 223 shows the fabric requirements for the base pattern for a skirt in your size. It is important also to consider any adaptations, variations and parts you draw yourself when determining the final amount of fabric needed for your project. Remember to allow extra fabric for the wrap.

Extras
- Fusible interfacing for the waistband
- Hook-and-eye or snap fastener

Fabric suggestions
We recommend a lightweight viscose, crepe or linen fabric if opting for a summer skirt or a firm medium-weight fabric for a more structured look.

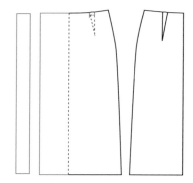

Pattern pieces

PATTERN PIECE	CUTTING INSTRUCTIONS
Skirt front piece ✎	Cut 2
Skirt back piece	Cut 1 on the fold
Facing front piece ✎	Cut 2
Waistband part A ✎	Cut 1 on the fold + 1 in interfacing
Waistband part B ✎	Cut 1 on the fold + 1 in interfacing
Tie band ✎	Cut 2

Variations

Length
The pattern pieces are marked mini and midi length, but create your desired length by measuring from the waist down. Remember to add 4 cm (1½ in) for the hem.

Skirt edge
You can vary the front edge in different ways. Cut it straight, curved or diagonally, depending on the desired look. If you decide on a curved or ruffled skirt edge, we recommend finishing the edge with a double hem and topstitching it in place rather than adding a facing.

Ruffle
Adding a ruffle can give the skirt a more romantic look. Attach the ruffle along the bottom edge, or curve the edge of the right front piece to start the ruffled edge from the waist. To avoid creating volume under the skirt, we recommend finishing the ruffle at the bottom corner of the left front piece. See page 198 for how to make a ruffle.

Pattern adjustments

Wrap

For the wrap on the front piece, extend the front edge of the pattern by 15 cm (6 in) from the centre front. Vary the shape of the front by drawing a diagonal or curved line from the waist to the hemline. Experiment with different angles.

Facing

Draw a facing 7 cm (2¾ in) wide for the centre front of both sides of the front piece. See page 174 for how to draw a facing. If you want to add a ruffle along the skirt edge, a facing is not necessary.

Waistband

The waistband consists of two parts, A and B, both 10 cm (4 in) high. We recommend making the waistband parts after you have sewn darts and pleats on the skirt and sewn the side seam, as it is easier to take correct measurements.

Part A: Measure the length from the left side seam to the end of the left front piece. Add 2 cm (¾ in) for seam allowances (1 cm/⅜ on each side).

Part B: Measure the length from the left side seam to the outer edge of the right front piece. Add 2 cm (¾ in) for seam allowances (1 cm/⅜ in each side).

Tie bands

The measurement for each tie band is 10 x 50 cm (4 x 20 in).

Before you begin:

Iron interfacing onto the waistband pieces. Finish all raw edges by sewing a zigzag or overlock stitch around the pattern pieces.

Sewing instructions

1.

Darts and pleats
Sew darts on the back piece according to the marking on the pattern. On the front pieces, the marked darts should be sewn as pleats. The dart width indicates the width of the pleat. Fold the pleat towards the centre front. See pages 184–187 for how to sew darts and pleats.

2.

Side seams
Place one front piece and the back piece right sides together, align the side edges and sew the side seam. Press the seam open. Repeat for the other side.

3.

Facing
Place one facing piece on the corresponding front piece, right sides together, and secure with pins. Sew along the entire edge and press the facing towards the inside of the skirt. Secure the facing on the inside of the skirt by sewing it to the seam allowance. Repeat for the other front piece.

If you are sewing a skirt with a ruffle or shaped edge you can omit this step. Instead, either add the ruffle or fold a double hem and topstitch in place

4.

Tie bands
Sew tie bands following the instructions on page 210. Since the tie bands will be sewn into the waistband, leave one short side open and secure the seam allowance with an overlock or zigzag stitch after turning the tie band right side out.

5.

Waistband
Fold both waistbands lengthwise, wrong sides together, and press so that you have a crease along the centre of each waistband.

→ *Wrap skirt with bias edge and long ruffle combined with swimsuit on page 147.*

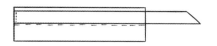

With part A right side facing you, place the zigzagged end of one tie band aligned with the short raw edge on the left side. The tie band should be placed just above the crease. See illustration for placement.

Place part B onto part A, right sides together, so that the raw edges on the left side are aligned with the tie band in between. Pin and sew together. Press the seam open.

Unfold part B. Place the other tie band right sides together on part B of the waistband, so the zigzagged end is aligned with the other short raw edge. The tie band should be placed right up against the crease. Pin or tack (baste) in place.

Fold the waistband lengthwise with wrong sides together, and sew along side edges. Turn right side out – one tie band will be attached to the right side edge and the other will be attached between the middle and left side.

Press the lower edge of the waistband (on the side without the tie bands) by 1 cm (⅜ in) towards the wrong side.

6.

Place the waistband, right sides together, onto the top edge of the skirt. Start at the end of the left wrap and work your way around pinning the waistband in place. The tie band sewn between parts A and B should match up with the left side seam. The tie band sewn onto the end of part B will extend from the right front piece. Sew the waistband in place and press the seam allowance towards the waistband.

Fold the waistband over to the wrong side and pin the pressed edge to the lower edge from the right side. Stitch from the right side in the crease from the previous seam so that the seam is invisible from the right side. Make sure to catch the inner waistband in the seam

7.

Hem
Fold the hemline of the skirt up by 1 cm (⅜ in) and then by 3 cm (1¼ in). Topstitch or slip stitch in place. See page 166 for how to slip stitch. If you are sewing a skirt with a curved or ruffled edge you can omit this step.

8.

Sew a snap fastener or hook-and-eye on the inside of the waistband, aligning it with the right side seam for secure the wrap on the inside of the skirt.

Wide-leg trousers (pants) are a timeless wardrobe classic that can be worn for most occasions. We love that they are comfortable to wear, yet effortlessly stylish, and create an elongated silhouette that flatters all body shapes. Our version features pleats in the waist, and you can choose to sew them with or without a fly. Style them with various tops and accessories to create different looks for different occasions.

Trousers

You will need

Fabric
The table on page 223 shows the fabric requirements for the base pattern for trousers in your size. It is important also to consider any adaptations, variations and parts you draw yourself when determining the final amount of fabric needed for your project.

Extras
- Interfacing for waistband and fly facing
- Button
- Invisible zip for side closure (30 cm/12 in) or regular zip for fly front zip (20 cm/8 in)

Fabric suggestions
We recommend medium-weight smooth wool or cotton twill for smooth elegance. Go with lightweight linen or crepe for a more summery vibe.

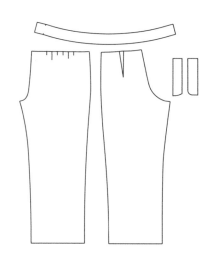

← *Trousers in silk combined with shirt on page 47.*

Pattern pieces

PATTERN PIECE	CUTTING INSTRUCTIONS	
	Side closure	*Fly front zip*
Trouser front piece	Cut 2	Cut 2
Trouser back piece	Cut 2	Cut 2
Waistband	Cut 2 + 2 in interfacing	Cut 2 + 2 in interfacing
Fly (facing)		Cut 1 + 1 in interfacing
Fly (flap)		Cut 1 + 1 in interfacing

Variations

Length
Alter the trousers to your perfect length, including as shorts. Use the hip or knee line as a starting point when calculating the length. Measure yourself first and then adjust the pattern pieces accordingly.

Fit
For narrower trousers, draw a diagonal line from the hip marking down to the bottom hemline.

Closure
Chose a side closure with an invisible zip, or a centre front closure with a fly front zip.

Pockets
If you choose to use a fly front zip, you can add pockets to the side seams by following the instructions on page 200.

Iron interfacing to the waistband and, if necessary, to the fly facing. Finish all raw edges by sewing a zigzag or overlock stitch around the pattern pieces.

Sewing instructions

1.

Pleat
Sew the pleats on the front pieces according to the markings on the pattern. See page 186 for how to sew pleats

2.

Darts
Sew the darts on the back pieces according to the markings on the pattern. See page 184 for how to sew darts.

3.

For a side closure
Sew the zip in place, right sides together, at the top of the left front piece. The teeth of the zip should be placed 1 cm (⅜ in) from the top. Sew the other side of the zip to the left back piece in the same way. See page 178 for how to sew an invisible zip.

Skip this step for a fly front zip – it will be sewn in step 6.

4.

Side seams
Place one front piece and one back piece right sides together, and sew the side seam. For an invisible zip, sew up to the bottom point of the zip on the side with the zip. For a fly front zip, the side seam should be fully sewn. Repeat for the other leg and press the seam open.

Remember, if you want to add side pockets to the trousers (pants), you must sew them in when sewing the side seams. See page 200 for how to sew pockets.

5.

Inner seam
Place the pieces with right sides together again and sew the inner seam on each leg, then press the seam open.

6.

Fly front zip
Sew the fly piece at the top between the two front pieces following the instructions on page 180. Skip this step if you have sewn an invisible zip side closure.

7.

Turn one trouser leg right side out and place it inside the other trouser leg so that the crotch curves match up. Make sure the inner seam matches and sew along the crotch curve. For a fly front zip, sew to the bottom of the fly. For an invisible zip, sew the entire seam. Turn the trousers inside out and press the curved crotch seam.

8.

Waistband
Place the two waistband pieces right sides together, and sew along the short sides and top edge. Trim the corners and clip the curve if necessary. Turn the waistband right side out and press.

9.

Press the seam allowance along one side of the waistband by 1 cm (⅜ in) towards the wrong side. This will be the front of the waistband.

10.

Place the back of the waistband with the right side facing the wrong side of the trousers.

For a side closure Pin the waistband to the top edge of the skirt, starting from the zip on the front piece. The waistband should extend about 4 cm (1½ in) beyond the zip on the back piece.

For a fly front zip Pin the waistband to the top edge of the skirt, from the fly flap around to the opposite side.

Sew the waistband in place and press the seam allowance up towards the waistband.

11.

Turn the waistband to the right side. Topstitch along the folded edge of the waistband from the right side of the trousers.

For a side closure As you reach the extension on the back piece, fold the bottom edge by 1 cm (⅜ in) towards the wrong side to conceal the raw edge. Align the ends of the waistband and continue topstitching along the folded edge.

12.

Hem
Fold the hemline of the trousers up by 1 cm (⅜ in) and then by 3 cm (1¼ in). Topstitch or slip stitch in place. See page 166 for how to slip stitch.

13.

Buttonhole and button
Sew buttonholes with a sewing machine. With a side closure, the buttonhole is placed on the waistband above the zip on the front piece. The waistband extension on the back piece is placed under the buttonhole for the button. With a fly, the buttonhole is placed where the fly overlaps when the zip is closed. Place the buttons to match the buttonhole.

← *Trousers combined with T-shirt on page 61.*

A versatile everyday dress is a lifesaver on busy mornings. It's that go-to dress you can just slip into and feel fabulous, no matter what the occasion. It combines comfort with style, ensuring you always look well put together, whether at the office, on lazy away days or at a special event. The dress is based on our blouse pattern, but you will extend the front and back pieces to create a wide dress length. The waist is accentuated using a tie or a belt, which gives the dress a flattering shape. For an extra touch of romance, consider adding a ruffle at the hemline.

Everyday dress

You will need

Fabric
The table on page 223 shows the fabric requirements for the base pattern for a straight top in your size. It is important also to consider any adaptations, variations and parts you draw yourself when determining the final amount of fabric for your project. Remember to allow extra fabric to extend the length and for balloon sleeves.

Extras
- Interfacing for facings and cuffs
- Invisible zip (40 cm/16 in) or hook-and-eye

Fabric suggestions
We recommend a light- to medium-weight fabric such as silk, cotton satin, or viscose. Consider linen for a more structured look.

109

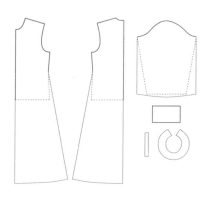

Pattern pieces

PATTERN PIECE	CUTTING INSTRUCTIONS
Straight top front piece ✎	Cut 1 on the fold
Straight top back piece ✎	Cut 1 – add seam allowance along the centre line
Straight sleeve ✎	Cut 2
Cuff	Cut 2 + 2 in interfacing
Neckline facing ✎	Cut 1 on the fold + 1 on the fold in interfacing
Belt loops ✎	Cut 2
Tie band ✎	Cut 1

Pattern adjustments

Facing
Draw a 6 cm (2⅜ in) wide neckline facing. See page 174 for instructions.

Balloon sleeves
Use the straight sleeve pattern to make a balloon sleeve with volume at the bottom. See page 217 for instructions.

Lengthen the top to make a dress
To lengthen the front and back pieces, measure the desired length from the waist down. Then extend the pattern pieces along the centre edge from the waist down, adding a 2 cm (¾ in) hem. Draw a horizontal line to meet the bottom point at right angles, which becomes the bottom edge of the dress.

To also add extra width to the skirt, mark a new point 4.5 cm (1¾ in) outside the lower corner in the side seam. Then draw a diagonal line from the waist marking in the side seam out to this point and onward at the same angle until you hit the line you drew for the bottom edge of the dress.

Tie belt and belt loops
See page 210 for instructions. You need two belt loops, one in each side seam. You can also use a belt with a buckle instead of ties.

Variations

Neckline
The dress can be varied with different necklines. See page 220 for how to create different necklines.

Closure
The dress features a back closure. Choose whether to insert an invisible zip or make a slit with a hook-and-eye. If you make a neckline large enough to fit your head through, you can cut the back piece on the fold and skip the closure in the middle.

Decorative collar
The dress gets a little extra flair with a large collar. See page 208 for how to design your own decorative collar.

Ruffles
If you want a more romantic dress, it can be nice to add one or more ruffles down the length of the dress. See page 198 for how to make ruffles.

Elastic waistband
You can replace the tie belt with an elastic waistband as explained on page 214, or with shirring at the waist as explained on page 192.

Before you begin:

Iron interfacing onto the cuffs, facings, and optional decorative collar. Finish all raw edges by sewing zigzag or overlock stitches around the pattern pieces.

Sewing instructions

1.

Tie belt and belt loops
Sew the tie belt and belt loops following the instructions on page 210.

2.

Closure
For closure with invisible zip   Insert the zip between the two back pieces on the centre back seam. The teeth of the zip should start 1 cm (⅜ in) from the neck opening to allow for the facing. See page 178 for how to insert an invisible zip. Complete the centre back seam from the lower edge to the zip, and press open.

For a slit closure   Place the back pieces right sides together. Measure 20 cm (8 in) from the neckline down along the centre back seam and make a mark for the bottom of the slit. Sew the centre back seam from the lower edge to the mark. Press the seam open and the seam allowance on the slit towards the wrong side.

3.

Shoulder seams
Place the front and back pieces right sides together, and sew the shoulder seams. Press the seams open.

4.

Decorative collar (optional)
See page 208 for how to sew a decorative collar.

5.

Facing
Attach the facing, right sides together, to the neckline and sew in place. If you have included a decorative collar, place it between the facing and the neck opening. See page 174 for how to sew a facing with or without an invisible zip.

For a slit closure   Topstitch along the edges of the slit to secure the seam allowance. Sew a hook-and-eye at the top of the neck opening by hand.

6.

Sleeves
Fold each cuff lengthwise, wrong sides together, and press. Open out the cuff again and press one long edge 1 cm (⅜ in) towards the wrong side.

→   *Long everyday dress with a square neckline, deep ruffle and belt.*

7. Sew gathering stitches along the lower edge of both sleeves and gather the fabric to fit the width of the cuff. See page 188 for how to gather.

8. Attach the bottom edge of the sleeve to the unfolded edge of the cuff, right sides together, and sew to secure the gathers in place. Press the seam allowance towards the sleeve.

9. Place the dress with the right side facing you and pin one sleeve, right sides together, to the corresponding armhole. Sew in place and press the seam open. Repeat for the other sleeve.

10.

Side seams
Place the dress right sides together, aligning the side and sleeve edges. Attach the belt loops to the waist on each side, so that they lie between the front and back pieces. Sew together with a seam from the bottom edge of the cuff, under the armhole, and down to the hemline of the dress. Press the seam open. Repeat for the other side.

11.

Ruffle (optional)
Sew one or more ruffles to the skirt if desired. See page 198 for how to make a ruffle.

12. Fold the cuff over to the wrong side and sew the folded edge to the seam allowance between the sleeve and the cuff. Remove the gathering stitches.

13.

Hem
Fold and press the bottom edge 1 cm (⅜ in) towards the wrong side twice, so that the raw edge is hidden inside the fold. Topstitch from the right side.

The timeless and elegant wrap dress has been a favourite for many since it gained popularity in the 1970s. What we love most about it is its ability to make anyone feel confident, as it flatters all body types. The wrap and tie bands allow you to adjust it so that it sits perfectly at the waist and creates a feminine silhouette. It is versatile and smart and can easily be thrown over a swimsuit on the way home from the beach or dressed up for a party. You can vary the look with curved edges and romantic ruffles, or go for straight lines for a streamlined look. The dress is easy to sew as it does not require a zip closure or any intricate sewing details.

Wrap dress

You will need

Fabric
The table on page 223 shows the fabric requirements for the base pattern for a fitted top and skirt in your size. It is important also to consider any adaptations, variations and parts you draw yourself when determining the final amount of fabric for your project. Remember to allow extra fabric for the wrap.

Extras
- Hook-and-eye or snap fastener

Fabric suggestions
We recommend light- to medium-weight fabrics. Consider a structured jacquard for a stylish mini or soft viscose for an elegant maxi dress.

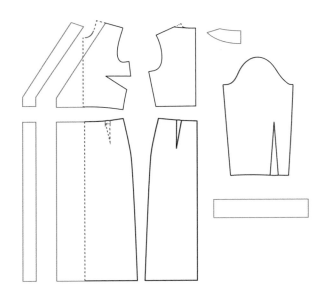

Pattern pieces

PATTERN PIECE	CUTTING INSTRUCTIONS
Fitted top front piece ✐	Cut 2
Fitted top back piece ✐	Cut 1 on the fold
Fitted sleeve ✐	Cut 2
Skirt front piece ✐	Cut 2
Skirt back piece ✐	Cut 1 on the fold
Tie band ✐	Cut 2
Neckline facing ✐	Cut 1 on the fold
Skirt facing ✐	Cut 2

Pattern adjustments

Wrap top

Front piece: Transfer the shoulder point from the pattern to mark the neckline. Extend the lower edge of the top by drawing a horizontal line 15 cm (6 in) from the bottom corner of the centre front. From this point, draw a vertical line straight up for 5 cm (2 in). From the end of this, draw a diagonal line to the new neckline point. If desired, you can create a more curved neckline based on the diagonal.

Back piece: Transfer the shoulder point from the pattern to mark the neckline. Create a new neckline by drawing a line from this point to the centre back, intersecting the original neckline.

Wrap skirt
To create extra width for the wrap on the front skirt, extend the front edge of the skirt by 15 cm (6 in) from the centre front. Vary the shape of the front by drawing a diagonal or curved line from the broadest point of the shoulder down to the hemline. Experiment with different angles.

Facing
Draw a facing 7 cm (2¾ in) wide for the front edges and neckline of the top and skirt. See the instructions for drawing the facing on page 174. If you have chosen a very delicate fabric, consider a double folded hem instead of a facing.

Sleeve
You can choose which sleeve variant you want to use on the dress. We have chosen balloon sleeves and short puff sleeves on our dresses. Use the fitted sleeve and see page 216 for various sleeve variations.

Tie bands
The measurement for each tie band is 10 x 50 cm (4 x 20 in).

Variations

Neckline
You can choose to make the neckline more or less curved when drawing the front piece.

Length
The pattern pieces are marked mini and midi length, but you can measure from the waist to your desired length, adding a 4 cm (1½ in) hem.

Skirt edge
You can vary the front edge in different ways. Cut it straight, curved or diagonally, depending on the desired look. If you decide on a curved or ruffled skirt edge, we recommend finishing the edge with a double-folded hem rather than a facing.

Ruffle
Adding a ruffle can give the skirt a more romantic look. Attach the ruffle along the bottom edge, or curve the edge of the right front piece to start the ruffled edge from the waist. To avoid creating volume under the dress, we recommend finishing the ruffle at the bottom corner of the left front piece. See page 198 for how to make a ruffle.

Finish all edges of the fabric pieces by sewing a zigzag stitch or using an overlock (serger) machine. It is not necessary to do this on the tie bands.

Sewing instructions

1.

Darts and pleats

Sew darts on the back piece according to the marking on the pattern. On the front pieces, the marked darts should be sewn as pleats. The dart width indicates the width of the pleat. Fold the pleat towards the centre front. See pages 184–187 for how to sew darts and pleats.

2.

Shoulder seams

With front and back top pieces right sides together and aligning shoulder edges, sew the shoulder seams. Press the seams open.

3.

Sleeves

Sew the sleeves according to your chosen style following the instructions on page 216.

4.

Place the top with the right side facing you and pin one sleeve, right sides together, to the corresponding armhole. Sew in place and press the seam. Repeat for the other sleeve.

5.

Tie bands

Sew tie bands following the instructions on page 210. Since the tie bands will be sewn into the waistband, leave one short side open and secure the seam allowance with an overlock or zigzag stitch after turning the tie band right side out.

Place one tie band on the extended edge of the right front top, aligning the zigzagged edge with the front edge and positioning it 1 cm (⅜ in) up from the bottom edge to allow for the seam allowance. Stitch in place using a seam allowance slightly less than 1 cm (⅜ in).

Place the other tie band on the side edge of the left front top, positioned as described above. Sew in place.

To check you have found the correct placement, place the right front top over the left to see if the tie bands meet so that they can be tied on the left side.

→ *Short wrap dress with short puff sleeves.*

6.

Side seams

Place the front and back pieces of the top right sides together, and sew the side seams from the bottom of the sleeve, under the armhole, and down to the hemline on each side.

Place the front pieces of the skirt onto the back piece, aligning the side edges, and sew the side seam.

Press the seams open.

7.

Pin the top and skirt right sides together, aligning the waistband edge and the side seams. Make sure the ties are facing upwards so that you don't catch them in the stitching. Sew the waistline seam and press it open.

8.

Facing

Sew the facing pieces together at the shoulders and at the waist to make a continuous strip. Press all the seams open.

Pin the facing, right sides together, onto the opening of the dress. Make sure the shoulder and waist seam match up, the front edge is aligned, and that the ties are positioned out of the way. Sew the facing in place and press it towards the wrong side of the dress. Secure the facing on the wrong side by sewing through the facing and seam allowance around the entire edge.

If you are sewing a skirt with a ruffle or shaped edge you can omit this step. Instead, either add the ruffle or fold a double hem and topstitch in place

9.

Hem

Fold and press the bottom edge 1 cm (⅜ in) towards the wrong side twice, so that the raw edge is hidden inside the fold. Topstitch from the right side. If you are sewing a skirt with a ruffle or shaped edge you can omit this step.

If you have chosen a sleeve variation without a cuff, hem the sleeve in the same way.

10.

Sew a snap fastener or a hook-and-eye on the inside of the dress, placed on the waist seam to secure the wrap on the inside.

The chic and understated style of the baby doll dress, with its fitted bodice and billowing tiered skirt, captures the essence of the Scandinavian aesthetic. It offers a perfect romantic summer look when paired with sandals, or for a trendy vibe you can layer it with jeans or a turtleneck sweater. Our baby doll dress has only two pattern pieces, combined with rectangles that you draw yourself. This makes it easy to vary both the length and volume of the ruffles and sleeves to suit your own taste.

Babydoll dress

You will need

Fabric
The table on page 223 shows the fabric requirements for the base pattern for a fitted top in your size. It is important also to consider any adaptations, variations and parts you draw yourself when determining the final amount of fabric. You will need lots of extra fabric for ruffles and puff sleeves.

Extras
- Interfacing
- Invisible zip (40 cm/16 in)
- Elastic (1 cm/⅜ in wide)

Fabric suggestions
We recommend a lightweight cotton satin or poplin fabric.

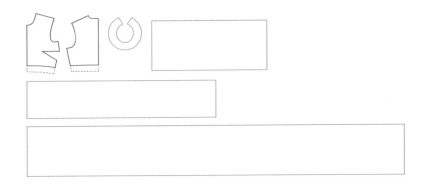

Pattern pieces

PATTERN PIECES	CUTTING INSTRUCTIONS
Fitted top front piece	Cut 1 on the fold
Fitted top back piece	Cut 2 – add seam allowance along the centre line
Sleeve 🖉	Cut 2
Ruffle 🖉	Cut 1 for each ruffle
Neckline facing 🖉	Cut 1 on the fold + 1 on the fold in interfacing

Variations

Neckline
The dress can be varied with different necklines. See page 220 for how to create different necklines.

Length
Change the dress length by varying the size and number of ruffles. Adjust the different rectangles that make up the skirt and add as many tiers as you want. We have used two ruffles.

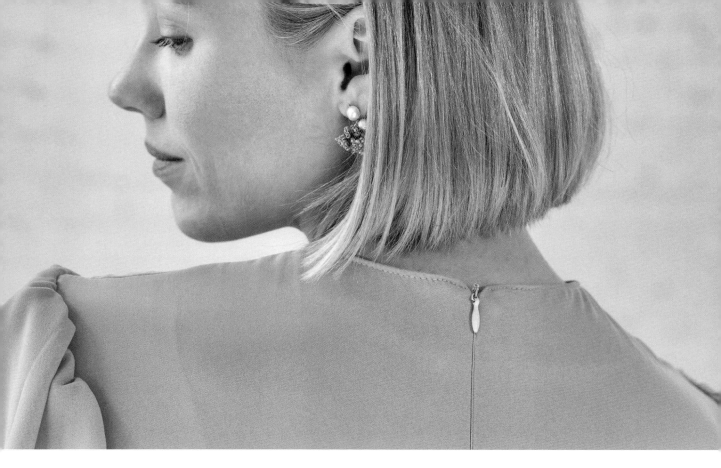

Pattern adjustments

Facing
Draw a 6 cm (2⅜ in) wide facing for the neckline. See page 174 for how to draw a facing.

Sleeve
For the sleeve, draw a rectangle with a width that corresponds to the circumference of the armhole on the pattern x 2. The length is up to you – we made our sleeve about 40 cm (16 in) long.

Ruffles
Draw rectangles for the desired number of ruffles on the skirt. Each tier should be twice as wide as the edge it is to be sewn onto, with the top tier matching the waistline x 2. You can sew strips of fabric together to get the desired width if necessary, but make sure that the seams are in line with the side seams of the top. The first tier must have a centre back seam to accommodate the zip. You can follow this on subsequent tiers, or have seams only at the sides. Adjust the depth of each tier to achieve your required dress length.

Iron the interfacing onto the facing. Finish all raw edges by sewing a zigzag or overlock stitch around the pattern pieces.

Sewing instructions

1.
Darts
Sew the darts on the front top according to the markings on the pattern. See page 184 for how to sew darts.

2.
Shoulder seams
Place the front and back pieces for the top right sides together, aligning shoulder edges, and sew the shoulder seams. Press the seams open.

3.
Side seams
Align the side edges and sew the side seams. Press the seams open.

4.
Tiered skirt
Join any pieces so that each ruffle becomes one long piece. Sew gathering stitches on the upper edge of each ruffle. See page 188 for how to gather.

Begin by gathering the first tier so that it fits the edge of the top. Pin the ruffle, right sides together, to the top matching side seams and sew together. Make sure the gathers are even. Remove any visible gathering stitches and press the seam allowance.

Repeat this to attach each tier to the one above.

5.
Zip closure
Insert the invisible zip along the centre back seam. The zip teeth should start 1 cm (⅜ in) from the neck opening to allow space for the facing. See page 178 for how to insert an invisible zip. Complete the centre back seam from the hemline to the zip. Press the seam open.

6.
Facing
Pin the facing to the neckline, right sides together, and sew it in place. See page 174 for how to sew a facing to a neckline with an invisible zip.

7.
Sleeves
Fold the sleeve lengthwise with right sides facing and aligning edges and sew together on the short edge. Press the seam open. Repeat for the other sleeve.

8. Sew gathering stitches along the upper edge of each sleeve. Gather the top of each sleeve to fit into the armhole. Sew in place.

9. Create a casing at the bottom edge of each sleeve and insert the elastic. Measure the elastic around your arm to determine the desired length before cutting. See page 214 for how to sew a casing with an elastic.

10. Turn the dress right side out and place one sleeve inside the dress, right sides together. Pin along the armhole and stitch the sleeve in place. Repeat for the other sleeve.

11. Fold and press the bottom edge 1 cm (⅜ in) towards the wrong side twice, so that the raw edge is hidden inside the fold. Topstitch from the right side.

The cocktail dress embodies classical elegance, making it perfect for any special occasion. Its flattering silhouette creates a sophisticated look that is always in fashion. Choose to keep it simple and timeless – the classic 'little black dress' – or play with vibrant hues and shimmering brocade for a glamorous interpretation. It lends itself to a variety of sleeve variations, from no sleeves to straight sleeves or puff sleeves. Either way it is a true staple in any wardrobe.

Cocktail dress

You will need

Fabric
The table on page 223 shows how much fabric you need for the base pattern for a fitted top and skirt in your size. When calculating the amount of fabric needed, you also need to consider any adjustments, variations, and self-drawn parts.

Extras
- Interfacing
- Invisible zip (minimum length 60 cm/24 in)

Fabric suggestions
We recommend using medium-weight fabrics such as silk, satin, velvet or brocade.

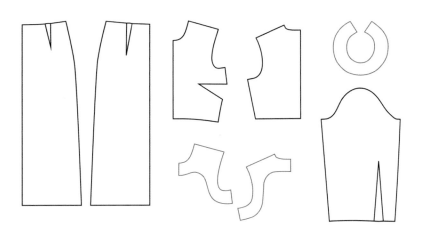

Pattern pieces

PATTERN PIECE	CUTTING INSTRUCTIONS	
	Sleeveless	*With sleeves*
Fitted top front piece	Cut 1 on the fold	Cut 1 on the fold
Fitted top back piece	Cut 2 – add seam allowance along the centre line	Cut 2 – add seam allowance along the centre line
Skirt front piece	Cut 1 on the fold	Cut 1 on the fold
Skirt back piece	Cut 2 – add seam allowance along the centre line	Cut 2 – add seam allowance along the centre line
Fitted sleeve		Cut 2
Neckline facing ✐		Cut 1 on the fold + 1 on the fold in interfacing
Combination facing ✐	Cut 1 + 1 in interfacing	

Pattern adjustments

Facing
Draw a 6 cm (2⅜ in) wide facing for the neckline. For the sleeveless version, you will also need a facing for the armhole. We recommend a combined facing rather than cutting separate neckline and armhole facings – see the illustration above. See page 174 for how to draw a facing.

Variations

Neckline
The dress can be varied with different necklines. See page 220 for how to create different necklines.

Length
The pattern pieces indicate mini and midi length, but create your desired length by measuring from the waist down. Remember to add 4 cm (1½ in) extra for the hem.

Sleeves
For a version with sleeves, use the fitted sleeve or change to your desired shape as shown on page 216.

Iron interfacing onto the facing pieces. Finish all raw edges by sewing a zigzag stitch or using an overlock machine (serger) around the pattern pieces.

Sewing instructions

1.

Darts
Sew darts on the front of the top and on the front and back skirt pieces according to the markings on the pattern. See page 184 for how to sew darts.

2.

Shoulder seams
Place the front and back top pieces right sides together, aligning shoulder seams, and sew the seams. Press the seams open.

3.

Facing
Pin the facing to the neck opening, right sides together, and sew in place. For a combination facing, first join the front and back facing at the armholes. Sew along the neckline and around the armholes and clip into any curves to reduce bulk. Turn the top right side out by gently pulling the back piece through the shoulders on each side. Press the facing flat.

4.

Side seams
Place the front and back pieces of the top right sides together, aligning side edges, and sew the side seams. If you are using a combination facing, fold out the facing and continue stitching to sew the side seam of the facing also.

Place the front and back skirt pieces right sides together, aligning side edges, and sew the side seams.

Press the seams open.

5.

Place the top and skirt right sides together, aligning the waistline and side seams, and sew together to assemble the dress. Press the seam open.

6.

Zip closure
Insert the invisible zip along the centre back seam. The zip teeth should start 1 cm (⅜ in) from the neck opening to allow space for the facing. See page 178 for how to insert an invisible zip.

Complete the centre back seam from the hemline to the zip. Press the seam open.

→ *Kristin in a short cocktail dress with leg of mutton sleeves and Oda in a sleeveless cocktail dress.*

7.

Sleeves
For a dress with sleeves, sew the sleeve darts as marked on the pattern or follow the instructions on page 216 for your chosen sleeve shape. Fold the sleeve lengthwise, right sides together aligning edges, and sew the centre seam. Press the seam open. Repeat for the other sleeve.

Turn the dress inside out and place one sleeve inside the dress, right sides together. Pin the sleeve to the armhole and sew it in place. Press the seam open. Repeat for the other sleeve.

8.

Hem
Fold and press the bottom edge 1 cm (⅜ in) towards the wrong side twice, so that the raw edge is hidden inside the fold. Topstitch from the right side.

For a sleeve with no cuff, fold and press the hem by 1 cm (⅜ in) twice towards the wrong side. Topstitch from the right side.

Did you know that the jumpsuit has its origins in the practical outfit used by skydivers during daring jumps from planes? Since its introduction to the fashion world in the 1930s, jumpsuits for women have undergone a transformation, and now offer an array of styles and variations. What was once a daring statement piece has become a wardrobe staple, with people owning multiple versions. The beauty of the jumpsuit lies in its ability to provide a complete outfit in a single garment. Style it with sneakers for a comfortable everyday look, or dress it up with high heels for instant party glam.

Jumpsuit

You will need

Fabric
The table on page 223 shows how much fabric you need for the base pattern for a fitted top and trousers in your size. When calculating the fabric requirements, you also need to consider any adjustments, variations, and parts you draw yourself.

Extras
- Interfacing for facings and waistband
- Invisible zip (minimum length 60 cm/24 in)

Fabric suggestions
We recommend a light- to medium-weight linen or cotton fabric. Consider crepe or denim for a different look.

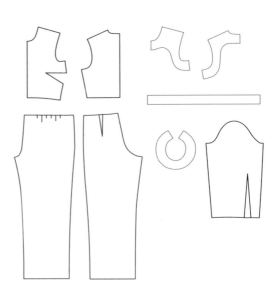

Pattern pieces

PATTERN PIECE	CUTTING INSTRUCTIONS	
	Sleeveless	*With sleeves*
Fitted top front piece	Cut 1 on the fold	Cut 1 on the fold
Fitted top back piece	Cut 2 – add seam allowance along the centre line	Cut 2 – add seam allowance along the centre line
Trouser front piece	Cut 2	Cut 2
Trouser back piece	Cut 2	Cut 2
Fitted sleeve		Cut 2
Neckline facing ✎		Cut 1 on the fold + 1 in interfacing
Combination facing ✎	Cut 1 + 1 in interfacing	
Waistband ✎	Cut 1 + 1 in interfacing	Cut 1 + 1 in interfacing

Pattern adjustments

Facing
Draw a 6 cm (2⅜ in) wide facing for the neckline. For the sleeveless version, you will also need a facing for the armhole. We recommend a combined facing rather than cutting separate neckline and armhole facings – see the illustration above. See page 174 for how to draw a facing.

Waistband
The waistband between the top and trouser pieces should be 6 cm (2⅜ in) high and as wide as the length along the top edge of the trousers/bottom edge of the top after darts and seams are sewn. We recommend cutting the waistband after other pieces are sewn together for exact measurements.

Variations

Neckline
The jumpsuit can be varied with different necklines. See page 220 for how to create different necklines.

Sleeves
For a version with sleeves, use the fitted sleeve or see page 216 for how to change the sleeve to your desired shape.

Tie belt
Consider adding a tie belt and belt loops to your jumpsuit. See pages 210–213 for how to sew a tie belt and belt loops.

Iron interfacing to the facings and waistband. Finish all raw edges by sewing a zigzag or overlock stitch around the pattern pieces.

Sewing instructions

1.

Darts
Sew darts on the front of the top and trouser (pants) back piece following the markings on the pattern. See page 184 for how to sew darts.

2.

Pleats
Sew pleats on the front of the trousers following the markings on the pattern. See page 186 for how to sew pleats.

3.

Shoulder seams
Place the front and back pieces of the top right sides together, and sew the shoulder seams. Press the seams open.

4.

Facing
Pin the facing to the neckline, right sides together, and sew. For a combination facing, first join the front and back facing at the armholes. Sew along the neckline and around the armholes and clip into any curves to reduce bulk. Turn the top right side out by gently pulling the back piece through the shoulders on each side. Press the facing flat.

5.

Side seams
Place the front and back pieces of the top right sides together aligning side edges, and sew the side seams. If you are using a combination facing, fold out the facing and continue stitching to sew the side seam of the facing also.

Place the trouser back piece on the corresponding front piece, right sides together and aligning side edges, and sew the side seam. Repeat for the other leg.

Press the seams open.

6.

Inner seam
With right sides still together, sew the inner seam of the leg. Repeat for the other leg. Press the seams open.

→ *Jumpsuit with short puffed sleeves.*

7.

Turn one trouser leg right side out and place it inside the other leg, right sides together. Sew the crotch seam from the top front to about 10 cm (4 in) into the back piece. This seam is finished after the zip is inserted.

8.

Waistband

Place the bottom edge of the waistband right sides together against the waistline of the trousers. Sew around the waistline.

Then attach the waistline of the top along the upper edge of the waistband, right sides together, and sew.

Press both seam allowances towards the waistband.

9.

Zip closure

Insert the invisible zip along the centre back seam. The zip teeth should start 1 cm (⅜ in) from the neck opening to allow space for the facing. See page 178 for how to insert an invisible zip.

Complete the crotch seam from where you left off in step 7 up to the bottom of the zip. Press the seam open.

10.

Sleeves

For a jumpsuit with sleeves, sew the sleeve darts as marked on the pattern or follow the instructions on page 216 for your chosen sleeve shape. Fold the sleeve lengthwise, right sides together aligning edges, and sew the centre seam. Press the seam open. Repeat for the other sleeve.

Turn the jumpsuit inside out and place one sleeve inside the top, right sides together. Pin the sleeve to the armhole and sew. Press the seam open. Repeat for the other sleeve.

11.

Hem

Fold and press the bottom edge 1 cm (⅜ in) towards the wrong side twice, so that the raw edge is hidden inside the fold. Topstitch from the right side.

For a sleeve with no cuff, fold and press the hem by 1 cm (⅜ in) twice towards the wrong side. Topstitch from the right side.

All women deserve a perfect and flattering swimsuit, in which they can feel comfortable both when lounging on the beach or swimming. Our swimsuit design embodies a straight and sporty style, perfect for a dip in a secluded mountain lake or soaking up the sun on a tropical beach. Style it with our wrap skirt, and you're dressed to have lunch at the beach restaurant or stroll home after a long day in the sun. The swimsuit is made in double layer fabric and finished with binding, so that all raw edges are hidden on the inside.

Swimsuit

You will need

Fabric
The table on page 223 shows how much fabric you need for the base pattern for a swimsuit in your size.

Fabric suggestions
We recommend choosing a medium-weight four-way stretch fabric, such as Lycra.

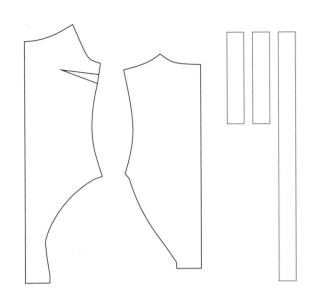

Pattern pieces

PATTERN PIECE	CUTTING INSTRUCTIONS
Swimsuit front piece	Cut 2 on the fold
Swimsuit back piece	Cut 2 on the fold
Binding and straps ✐	Cut 4

Measuring

Binding and straps
The binding is used to neaten the edges of the upper part of the swimsuit and extends to straps. Since the fabric already has a lot of stretch, cutting on the bias is not necessary. You need binding 4 cm (1½ in) wide in three different lengths:

Back binding: measure the centre back curved edge – cut 1
Front binding: measure the centre front curved edge – cut 1
Armhole binding: start with a length of 60 cm (24 in) to adjust later – cut 2.

Variations

A reversible swimsuit
Choose lining fabric in a different colour to the outer fabric, so that the swimsuit can be worn either way giving you two different looks.

Before you begin

The swimsuit is sewn inside out before being bagged out and finished with binding, so there is no need to finish raw edges before sewing. It is important to use an overlock machine (serger) or zigzag stitch when sewing all seams on the swimsuit (unless otherwise specified). This is to maintain the elasticity of the garment.

Sewing instructions

1.

Darts
Sew the darts on the front piece following the markings on the pattern. See page 184 for how to sew darts.

2.

Side seams
Place the front and back pieces right sides together aligning side edges, and sew the side seams.

3.

Repeat steps 1 and 2 on the lining fabric.

4.

Leg openings
With the wrong sides of both the outer and lining fabrics both facing out, align the left leg opening edges right sides together. Make sure the side seams are matching. Sew along the edge to join the outer and lining fabric around the left leg opening.

Repeat for the right leg. The centre seams should remain open for now.

5.

Turn the swimsuit with the back piece facing up. Place your hand through the open bottom of the back piece and take hold of the bottom of the front piece. Pull the front back into the opening of the back piece, aligning edges. Sew a seam straight across all four layers; this will be the crotch seam.

6.

Turn the entire swimsuit right side out by pulling it through the top edge of the back piece.

7.

Pin the two layers at the top of the swimsuit together and zigzag or overlock around the top edge.

8.

Edging
Attach the binding to the centre front and back curved edges using an elastic straight stitch on your machine. While sewing, stretch the binding slightly to ensure it follows the edges nicely. See page 190 for how to sew bias binding. Trim any excess binding.

9.

You will now attach the binding to the armholes and extend it to form a strap. Start by stitching the binding from the centre armhole along the back piece until you overlap the binding at the centre back. Remember to stretch the binding slightly as you stitch.

To determine the length of the strap, try on the swimsuit and pull the strap over your shoulder from the back. Use a pin to mark on the strap where you want it to meet the front. Measure the distance between the back piece and the pin for when you sew the opposite strap.

Sew the binding to the top of the front piece armhole, starting from the pin on the strap. Stitch along the front armhole. Overlap the binding in the centre to enclose all raw edges.

Topstitch the edge to secure the binding on both sides, making sure both raw edges are hidden inside. Maintain the same width for the straps as on the armhole edge.

Repeat for the opposite side.

A baguette bag is a stylish and practical accessory that exudes charm with its compact size. Its popularity soared in the late 1990s when Carrie Bradshaw fell in love with Fendi's iconic baguette bag in 'Sex and the City'. It gets its name from the short strap that allows it to be carried just under the arm, reminiscent of how the French carry baguettes. It can be made in many different materials, and a bold and colourful bag is an excellent way to elevate an outfit, making it a good choice for those looking to make a style statement.

Baguette bag

You will need

Fabrics
To sew this bag, you will need 0.5 m (20 in) of both outer fabric and lining fabric.

Extras
- 2 D-rings or other metal rings
- Zip (25 cm/10 in)
- Bias binding and piping cord (2 m/2¼ yd) – optional

Tip! *If you use a separating zip, it will be even easier to sew around the bag when joining the lining and outer fabric in step 8.*

Fabric suggestions
We recommend choosing a medium- to heavyweight fabric for the outer bag. For the lining, a lightweight cotton is a good choice.

153

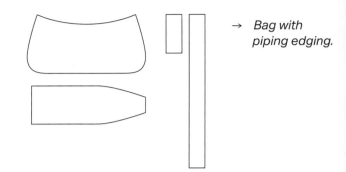

→ *Bag with piping edging.*

Pattern pieces

PATTERN PIECE	CUTTING INSTRUCTIONS
Baguette bag side	Cut 2 in the outer fabric + 2 in lining fabric
Baguette bag bottom	Cut 1 in the outer fabric + 1 in lining fabric
Baguette bag ring tab	Cut 2 on the fold in outer fabric
Baguette bag handle	Cut 1 on the fold in outer fabric

Variations

Handle or strap

For a shoulder bag with a longer strap, simply extend the handle to your desired length. You can also vary the look by attaching a chain, handle or strap that you already have instead of making the handle.

Piping

You can sew piping into the seams of the bag to create a contrasting detail. Piping is made by opening out bias binding and inserting piping cord. The bias binding is folded back around the cord and then placed on the right side of one of the fabric pieces, with raw edges aligned, before the seam to join two pieces is sewn. Sew with a zip foot to get as close to the piping cord as possible. When the piece is turned right side out, the piping stands out from the seam. If you don't want to make your own piping, it can be bought ready-made in a range of colours.

Before you begin

Finish all raw edges by sewing a zigzag or overlock stitch around them.

Sewing instructions

1.

Attach the bottom along the outer edge of one side piece with pins, right sides together. The bottom should go all the way around the bag, except for the top edge. Sew together.

If you want to add piping, do this before sewing the seams.

For a smooth seam on the curves, it may be helpful to hand-tack (baste) the pieces together around the most curved areas before sewing them with a machine.

Then attach the other side piece to the other side of the bottom and sew in the same way.

2.

Ring tab
Fold both long sides of the ring tab by 1 cm (⅜ in) towards the wrong side and press. Fold the tab lengthwise, wrong sides together, and press flat. Topstitch along the edge.

3.

Thread a D-ring onto the tab and fold it in half. Place the tab right sides together at the top of one short side of the bag. The fold with the D-ring should point downwards, so the raw edges are aligned at the top. Secure well with a seam back and forth along the raw edge.

Repeat steps 2 and 3 for the other ring tab.

4.

Zip
Cut the fabric tape of the zip at each end to the same length as the zip. Slightly burn the ends to prevent fraying.

5.

With the bag still wrong side out, place the zip right side down into the opening so the right sides are together. You can also choose to add piping between the zip and the bag at this stage. Pin the zip tape to the bag on each side of the opening and sew it in place along both edges. Open the zip.

6.

Lining
Assemble the lining as for the outer bag, omitting any piping and leaving about 5 cm (2 in) open in the centre of one side. Turn right side out.

7.

Place the lining inside the bag with right sides together, and pin it to the outer fabric with raw edges aligned around the entire opening. The zip and D-ring tabs are now between the lining and outer fabric. Sew around the edge.

8.   Carefully turn the bag right side out through the opening in the lining. Close the opening using ladder stitch. See page 168 for how to slip stitch.

9.   **Handle**
Fold both long sides of the handle by 1 cm (⅜ in) towards the wrong side and press. Then fold the handle lengthwise with wrong sides together and press flat. Topstitch along the edge.

10.   Attach the handle to the D-ring on each side of the bag by folding each end around and sewing back and forth over the handle.

The beret has a rich military history – it was originally part of the uniform of French troops, but towards the end of the 19th century it was embraced by artists and intellectuals in Paris. This simple but impactful accessory radiates sophistication and charm, with its round, flat crown and soft, slouchy brim. Whether worn tilted for a chic appearance or pulled straight for timeless style, it will add style to any outfit.

Beret

You will need

Fabric
To sew this beret you will need approximately 0.5 m (20 in) of both outer fabric and lining fabric.

Extras
- Bias binding for edging (optional)

Fabric suggestions
The beret was originally made of wool felt, but you can use other wool fabrics.

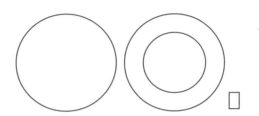

Pattern pieces

PATTERN PIECE	CUTTING INSTRUCTIONS
Beret top piece ✎	Cut 1 in outer fabric + 1 in lining fabric
Beret bottom piece ✎	Cut 1 in outer fabric + 1 in lining fabric
Beret stem ✎	Cut 1 in outer fabric

Pattern adjustments

Top and bottom
Draw two circles with a radius of 15 cm (6 in). On the bottom circle, draw an inner circle equal to the circumference around your head and then cut out the inner circle.

To calculate the radius of the inner circle, divide the head circumference by 3.14 and then divide the result by 2:
Radius = circumference around the head ÷ 3.14 ÷ 2.
Example: 58 cm ÷ 3.14 ÷ 2 = 9.2 cm
Example: 23 in ÷ 3.14 ÷ 2 = 3.6 in

Stem
Draw a rectangle measuring 5 x 3 cm (2 x 1¼ in) for the characteristic stem.

Variations

Lining or bias binding
Consider using bias binding for the edging as an alternative to lining the beret. Cut the bias binding to a length slightly longer than your head circumference and use it to finish the edge of the beret. This provides a decorative and stylish touch to the design.

Finish all edges by zigzag stitching or overlocking around the pattern pieces. You don't need to finish the edges of the stem.

Sewing instructions

1.

Stem
Fold the stem lengthwise right sides together, and sew along the long and one short side. Clip the seam allowance and turn the stem right side out using a crochet hook or a rouleau turner. Cut the stem to about 2 cm (¾ in).

2.

Find the centre of the beret top by folding it double, wrong sides together, and then fold it once more to make a triangular shape. The point corresponds to the centre point. Hand sew the stem in place.

3.

Beret outer
Place the top and bottom pieces right sides together, aligning the outer edge, and sew around the edge. Clip the seam allowance and turn right side out. Press the edges so that the seams lie flat. If you are not adding a lining, consider binding the seam allowance.

4.

Lining
Repeat step 3 for the lining, but do not turn right side out.

5.

Place the lining around the beret so the fabrics are right sides together. Pin along the inner circle and sew around, leaving about 5 cm (2 in) open.

6.

Carefully turn the beret right side out through the opening in the seam. Tuck the lining to the inside and press. Use ladder stitch to close the opening in the lining. See page 168 for how to ladder stitch. Consider topstitching around the opening to keep the lining in place.

7.

If you have sewn the beret without lining, sew bias binding around the inner circle edge. See page 190 for how to sew bias binding.

→ *Beret with turtleneck sweater and dress on page 37, and coat on page 79.*

Seams and techniques

Here we show you two techniques for nearly invisible hand sewing. Slip stitch is particularly useful for creating an invisible hem, while ladder stitch is ideal for joining fabrics in hard-to-reach areas, such as the edges of an opening after it has been turned inside out.

Invisible hand sewing

Invisible hem with slip stitch

Double fold and press the hem, ensuring that the raw edges are concealed inside and you have a neat folded edge at the top.

1. Knot the thread and secure it by inserting the needle through the top folded edge from inside.

2. Pick up a few threads from the fabric you're attaching the hem to and pull the thread through.

3. Insert the needle into the folded edge again and bring it back out about 0.5 cm (¼ in) from where it was inserted.

4. Repeat steps 2 and 3 along the folded edge, taking care not to pull the thread too tightly, as this can make the stitches more visible.

Tip! *Some sewing machines have a setting for sewing a similar hem, often called a blind hem. This can be a good alternative for thicker fabrics, but it can be more difficult to get the stitches completely invisible.*

Pressing the edges of each side of the fabrics you are joining makes stitching easier, but this may not always be feasible. If you don't have an edge on each side, you need to pay attention to where you insert the needle through the fabric and try sewing with even stitches throughout the process.

Closing an opening with ladder stitch

1.

First knot the end of the thread and secure it on the reverse of one of the fabrics by inserting the needle from the inside.

2.

Next, insert the needle into the opposite fabric, and pull the thread across. Bring the needle out about 3 mm (⅛ in) above where it was inserted and cross over to the opposite side again, using the same stitch length. Repeat this process several times to create a ladder-like stitch between the fabrics.

3.

When you pull the thread, the stitches will tighten, making the seam invisible from the right side.

[2]

[3]

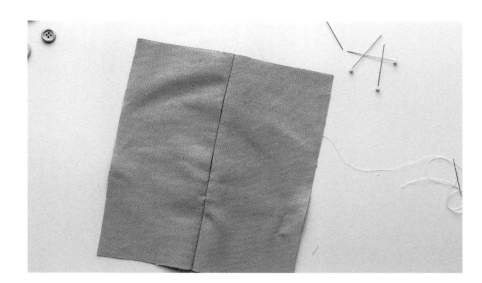

169

In a French seam, the raw edges are protected and concealed within the seam. This technique is particularly useful for delicate or lightweight fabrics where visible overlock or zigzag stitching would be undesirable.

French seam

1. Place the fabric pieces wrong sides together. Sew a smaller seam allowance than the one specified in the pattern, such as 0.5 cm (¼ in) instead of 1 cm (⅜ in).

2. Trim the seam allowance to 2–3 mm (⅛ in) and press the seam open.

3. Fold the fabric along the seam line, bringing the right sides together. Press the fold with an iron to create a crisp edge and secure it with pins.

4. Sew a new seam with a 0.5 cm (¼ in) seam allowance from the fold. This will enclose the raw edge inside the seam.

5. Press the seam to one side.

[2]

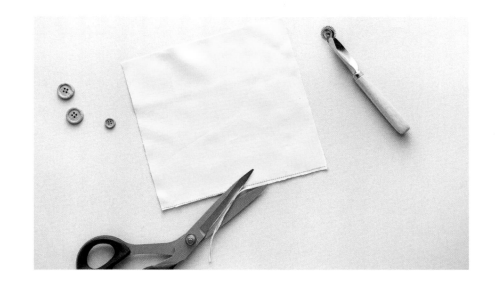

[3]

[5]

Sewing buttonholes on a sewing machine

Most newer sewing machines have a function for sewing buttonholes. The procedure may vary slightly from machine to machine, and instructions on how to sew buttonholes can be found in the sewing machine manual. However, we thought we would share some general tips for succeeding with buttonholes.

Buttons and buttonholes

1. Be careful with the placement of the buttonholes. This is especially important when you are sewing a row of them. Make sure they are placed in line and spaced an equal distance apart. Mark the placement of the buttonholes on the garment before you begin.

2. Make sure that the buttonhole is not placed too close to the edge of the fabric. A rule of thumb is that it should not be placed closer to the fabric edge than half the diameter of the button. This ensures that the button will fit comfortably through the hole and sit securely.

3. After machine sewing a buttonhole, it needs to be cut open. The most effective way is to use a seam ripper to cut into the fabric, but be careful not to cut the stitches. It can be helpful to place a pin horizontally at the end of the buttonhole to prevent the seam ripper from cutting too far.

4. It's important to sew the holes before attaching the buttons, to ensure even buttoning. If you sew the holes first, you can use them to determine button placement.

Sewing on buttons by hand

Buttons come in all shapes and colours and can change the look of a garment. Sometimes it may be wise to wait until the garment is finished before deciding which buttons to use. Then you can lay the different options on the fabric to see which looks best.

1. Use about 1 m (40 in) of thread, fold it in half and double it through the eye of the needle so that you are sewing with four threads. Tie a knot at the end.

2. Insert the needle through the fabric from the back and out through one of the holes in the button. To create some space between the button and the fabric, it can be a good idea to place a matchstick (or similar) under the button before you take the needle back down through the other hole. This allows room for an extra layer of fabric when the garment is closed.

3. After sewing a few stitches up and down through the holes of the button, insert the needle through the fabric from the back without passing it through the button, so that the thread is at the back of the button. Remove the matchstick and then wrap the thread 3–4 times around the stitches below the button to create a 'shank'.

4. Take the needle through to the back of the fabric and secure the thread by taking the needle through the stitches on the back of the fabric several times.

[1]

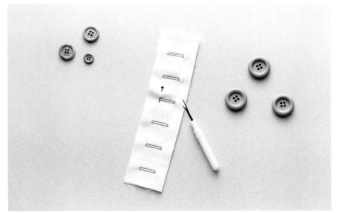

Sewing buttonholes on a sewing machine

[2]

Sewing on buttons by hand

A facing is a piece of fabric that is intended to be placed on the inside of a garment and used to create finishes along openings, such as a neckline or an armhole. The facing provides support to the garment and neatly finishes and conceals the raw edge. You can create facings yourself based on all the pattern pieces in the book and use them for any desired openings. Here, we will show you how to create a neckline facing and attach it to the garment.

Facing

1. To avoid cutting the facing in several parts, trace it from the front and back pieces as one piece. Place the pattern pieces for the front and back so that they overlap each other by 1 cm (⅜ in) at the shoulder seam (to exclude seam allowances). Mark a line on the pattern pieces 6 cm (2⅜ in) from the neckline. Make sure the line follows the same shape as the neckline.

2. Cut the facing following the instructions provided on the pattern piece it is based on, such as cutting on the fold. Reinforce it with interfacing on the wrong side and finish the edge with an overlock or zigzag stitch.

3. Align the right sides of the facing with the neckline, and pin them together. Sew the facing to the neckline along the inner curve. Clip notches in the seam allowance to reduce bulk when turning the facing to the wrong side.

4. Press the facing towards the wrong side of the neckline, ensuring it remains invisible from the right side. If needed, secure the facing by hand-stitching it to the shoulder seams with a few stitches.

5. Press the facing towards the wrong side of the neckline so that it becomes invisible from the right side. If it does not stay in place, you can hand-stitch it to the seam allowance at the shoulder seam with a few stitches.

[1]

[2]

[3]

[4]

[5]

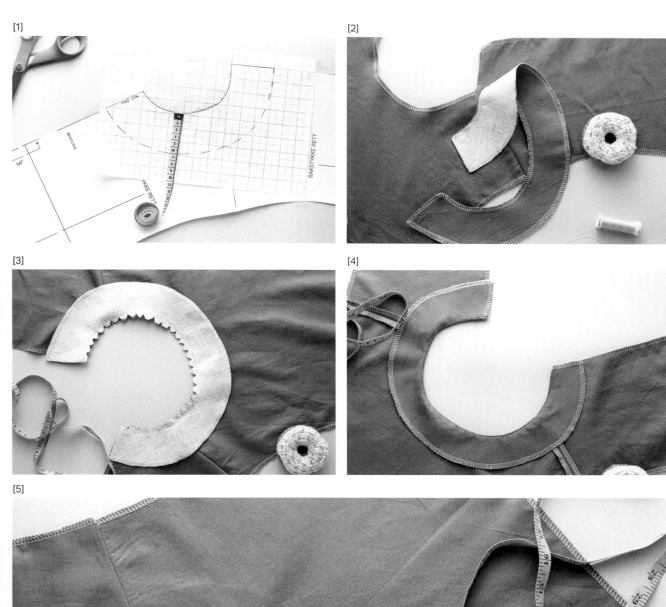
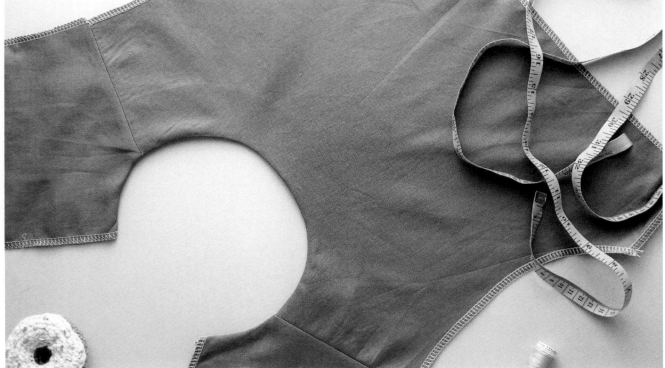

6.

Zip facing

To attach the facing to the zip seam allowance, fold out the zip tape and place the facing right sides together. Sew down the short edge of the facing just inside of the zip. Clip the corners.

When the facing is turned back towards the wrong side, the teeth of the zip will be facing out.

7.

Facing for other pattern pieces

You will also need to make facings for armholes and the opening along jackets and wrap-style garments. The same principles apply, but the instructions will specify if the facing should differ in appearance or be wider than 6 cm (2⅜ in) for that specific project.

An invisible zip is commonly used in dresses, skirts and trousers (pants) where you do not want a visible closure. By following this method, you can use either a zip foot and a standard foot on the sewing machine.

Invisible zip

1. Lay down the garment with the right side facing up.

2. Place the zip right side down on one side of the garment, with the edge of the zip tape aligned with the edge of the fabric. The teeth of the zip should start 1 cm (⅜ in) from the top edge to allow for the facing or waistband. Pin in place.

3. Sew the zip tape to the fabric using a zigzag stitch, but stop about 1 cm (⅜ in) before reaching the bottom of the zip pull. This makes it easier to make the zip completely invisible later on.

4. Fold out the zip teeth. Using a straight stitch, sew along the crease of the zip. The zizag stitch from step 3 will help keep the zip tape in place as you sew. Stop sewing 1 cm (⅜ in) above the zip pull.

5. Place the other side of the zip right sides together with the corresponding side of the garment. Repeat the same stitching process, ensuring to stop at the same point as the other side for a neat zip placement.

6. Close the zip and press well along the zip from both the right and wrong sides.

7. Place the two fabric pieces right sides together, and complete the seam up to where the zip ends. When you reach the bottom of the zip, adjust the needle position a couple of notches to the left. Sew diagonally along the zip until you overlap the zip seam.

8. Press the seam open and press over the zip and seam from the right side.

Tip! *A specific presser foot for invisible zips is available for most sewing machines, which can make the task even easier for you.*

[3]

[4]

[7]

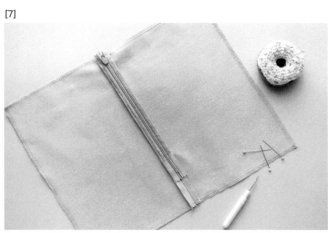

[8]

Here we show you how to use the pattern pieces to create a fly front zip in trousers (pants) or a skirt. For this you will need a visible zip that is 18–20 cm (7–8 in) long. The pattern pieces for the fly front can be found on the pattern sheet.

Fly front zip

1. Fold the flap right sides together and sew along the long side and the curved bottom edge with a 0.5 cm (¼ in) seam allowance. Clip into the seam allowance at the curve, turn the flap right side out and press. Topstitch along the curved edge. Iron interfacing onto the back of the facing and sew around the edge with an overlock or zigzag stitch.

2. Place the flap with the curved edge pointing to the right. Place the zip on the flap right side up, with the zip's seam allowance aligned with the left edge of the flap. Sew the zip onto the flap with a 0.5 cm (¼ in) seam allowance.

3. Open the zip and place the flap, right sides together, on the right front piece with the short top edge of the flap aligned with the top edge of the front piece. Sew with a 0.5 cm (¼ in) seam allowance, on top of the seam made in step 2. Close the zip when you have sewn a little over halfway, to make it easier to sew past the zip pull. The zip is now sandwiched between two fabric pieces.

4. From the right side, press a small fold from the front piece over the zip so it lies a few millimetres from the zip teeth. Use the zip foot to topstitch along the folded edge.

5. With the left front piece right side up, place the facing on top, right sides together, with the short edge of the facing aligned with the top edge of the front piece. Sew along the long edge of the facing with a 1 cm (⅜ in) seam allowance.

6. Press the facing to the wrong side of the front piece and sew a visible topstitch about 1–2 mm (¹⁄₁₆ in) from the fold to keep the facing on the inside.

[2]

[3]

[4]

[5]

[6]

7. Place the left front piece on top of the right front piece with right sides together. Sew up to where the fly starts. This will be the crotch seam for trousers (pants), and for skirts the front seam up from the bottom edge. Finish the seam just outside where you attached the facing (it can overlap by 1 cm/⅜ in).

8. Place the front piece right side up. Overlap the pieces in the opening as the fly will sit when closed (the zip should be hidden). Pin in place.

9. Turn the garment inside out, pin the loose side of the zip to the facing, and sew in place with a zip foot. Make sure you only sew through the facing and not the front piece.

10. From the wrong side: Sew the facing to the front piece from the wrong side using tacking (basting) stitches about 1 cm (⅜ in) from the edge of the facing (following the zigzag/overlock stitch on the facing). This will serve as a guide when you topstitch from the right side and will be removed at the end. Pin the fly to the right front piece so that you don't sew through it when you sew the stitches in the next step.

11. Turn to the right side and topstitch close to the tacking stitch. Sew slowly around the curve to make it as accurate and neat as possible. You can also sew an additional parallel line of topstitching 0.5 cm (¼ in) inside the first line to make the fly extra visible (as used on jeans). Remove the tacking stitches.

[7]

[8]

[9]

[10]

[11]

Darts are used to shape a flat piece of fabric into a three-dimensional form, ensuring a better fit around the body. They are commonly found around the waist of dresses and skirts, along the bust and armholes of tops, and occasionally around the shoulders or neckline. Proper use of darts will give a garment a flawless fit, and you can adjust them according to your measurements for a more personalised fit. In this book, you will encounter traditional darts that resemble a V shape, extending from the fabric's edge. When sewing darts, the aim is to create shape in the garment without adding unnecessary bulk. To achieve this, the dart's point should be virtually invisible, seamlessly blending with the fabric.

Darts

1. Transfer the marking of the dart from the pattern onto the wrong side of the fabric. See page 26 for tips on different marking tools.

2. Fold the fabric with right sides together, aligning the two end points of the dart. Pin along the dart, ensuring that the pin intersects the marked line on both sides of the fabric. Position the pin with its point facing towards the widest part of the dart.

3. Sew a straight line from the end of the dart down to the point. Secure the thread at both ends of the dart.

Pressing darts

4.

From the wrong side, use the iron on both sides of the dart to smooth out any wrinkles, before pressing the dart in the direction indicated in the instructions (usually towards the centre of the garment). Turn the fabric over and press from the right side so that the dart blends as seamlessly as possible into the fabric piece. Apply extra pressure to the bottom point of the dart so that it seems to blend in perfectly with the rest of the fabric.

Tip! *To avoid the dart from having a pointy shape, gently curve the seam a few millimetres at the very tip instead of sewing straight across, or stop machine stitching just before reaching the point and leave some extra thread to tie together at the end of the dart.*

[1]

[2]

[3]

[4]

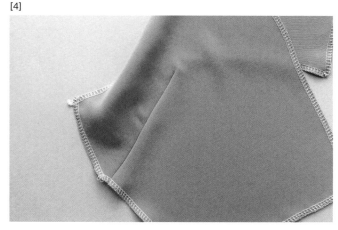

Pleats are created by making folds in the fabric that are pressed and stitched. This is a decorative and practical detail as it reduces the width of the fabric while allowing for ease of movement. On the trousers (pants) pattern, the pleats are marked with two parallel lines at the top of the front piece. One line indicates where to fold the fabric (foldline), while the other line shows where the folded edge should be placed. Generally, pleats should always be folded towards the centre of the garment.

Pleats

1. Cut notches or use pins to mark the lines that make up the pleat.

2. Place the piece with the right side facing you. Fold the fabric along the line closest to the side seam and then align this folded edge over the line closest to the centre. Secure with a pin.

3. Sew with a 0.5 cm (¼ in) seam allowance along the top edge of the piece to hold the folds in place. Press the fold flat.

[2]

[3]

187

Gathering is a technique used to reduce the length of a piece of fabric so that it can be sewn onto a shorter piece. It is often used to create volume or add decorative details, such as when making puffed sleeves, a full skirt, or adding ruffle details to a garment.

Gathering

1. Set the sewing machine to the maximum stitch length. Pull on the top and bobbin threads to ensure you have two tails of thread before starting to sew.

2. Sew a straight stitch about 0.5 cm (¼ in) from the raw edge, without securing the thread at the ends. At the end of the seam, cut the thread leaving a good length thread tail. Sew a new straight stitch parallel to the first one in the same way, 1.5 cm (⅝ in) from the edge.

3. Pull on the bobbin threads, at the same time moving the fabric along the stitching so that it gathers. Two parallel rows of gathering stitches give you more control over how the gathers lie. Take some time to make sure they are evenly distributed.

4. Once you have adjusted the length of the gathered fabric to match the piece you are attaching it to, pin the two fabric pieces together with their right sides facing. Sew them together using a regular stitch length and a 1 cm (⅜ in) seam allowance. This means you will sew between the two lines of gathering stitches, ensuring the gathers lie as desired.

5. Remove the gathering stitches with a seam ripper.

[2]

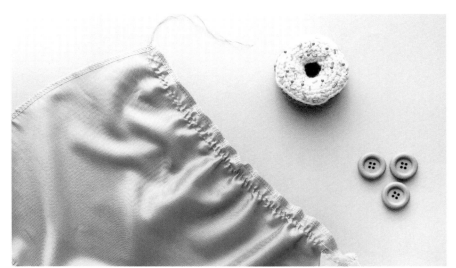

[3]

[4]

Bias binding or tape is a fabric strip cut on the bias and used as a finishing to conceal the raw edge of the fabric. It's a practical way to finish curved edges, which can be difficult to fold neatly. Ready-made bias binding is available in many different colours, patterns, widths and qualities, but it is also possible to make it yourself using a bias binding maker and an iron.

Bias binding

Making your own bias binding

1. Begin by determining the width of the binding according to your bias binding maker tool. For instance, if your bias binding maker is 18 mm (¾ in) wide, the fabric strip should be twice as wide, measuring 36 mm (1½ in).

2. Draw a square on your fabric following the grainlines and then draw diagonal lines at a 45-degree angle to the sides of the square. The distance between the lines should be equal to the width you determined in step 1.

3. Join the fabric strips together, as shown in the image, to create a long strip of fabric. Trim the seam allowances and press open.

4. Thread the strip into the bias binding maker – you can use a pin in the hole at the top to guide the fabric through. Pin the end of the bias binding to your ironing board and pull the bias binding maker backward while pressing the folded edges with an iron as the binding emerges.

To attach bias binding

5. Unfold one of the folded edges of the bias binding and align it with the raw edge on the wrong side of the fabric. The right side of the binding should face the wrong side of the fabric. Pin it in place.

6. Sew the tape to the fabric from the wrong side along the crease.

7. Fold the bias binding over the raw edge of the fabric, to bring it to the right side. Pin it in place so that the raw edge of the fabric is enclosed within the binding.

8. Topstitch from the right side of the fabric along the edge of the bias binding.

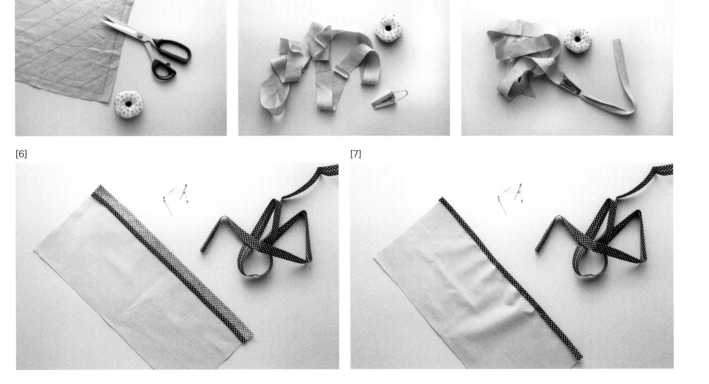

[2]

[3]

[4]

[6]

[7]

When machine sewing shirring, elastic thread is used as the bobbin thread. This specific thread creates a gathering effect in the fabric, resulting in a waffle-like texture and imparting elasticity to the areas where the stitches are formed. Shirring can therefore serve as an excellent alternative to cuffs or elastic waistbands. It is worth noting that shirring tends to work best on thin, lightweight fabrics, as thicker fabrics may not gather as effectively. The optimal settings for achieving the desired effect can also vary greatly depending on the machine and fabric being used. We strongly recommend conducting a test on a fabric scrap to fine-tune the settings on your machine before starting your project.

Shirring

1. Begin by manually threading the bobbin with slightly stretched elastic thread. Ensure that there is some tension in the elastic.

2. Thread the sewing machine, making sure that the elastic thread emerges through the needle plate.

3. Adjust the settings on your sewing machine. Generally, set the tension to a high level (around 6–8) and choose a long stitch length (approximately 4–5). Test these settings on a fabric scrap and make any necessary adjustments until you achieve the desired result. Ideally, the fabric should shrink to at least half of its original length.

4. Sew parallel lines of stitching with equal spacing to achieve a waffle pattern. It can be helpful to use the edge of the presser foot as a guide to sew the lines as straight as possible.

   Tip! *If you use a steam iron and press the seams lightly, you will see that the fabric shrinks even more.*

[1]

[3]

[4]

A vent in the back of a full-length coat provides more room for movement when walking and is also a detail that gives the coat a more tailored look. Here we show you how to sew a vent.

Vent

1. The left back piece should overlap the right back piece. On the right back piece, fold the hem up towards the right side by about 4 cm (1½ in) and sew a vertical stitch along the short side of the hem. Trim the corners and turn right side out.

2. Press the edge of the vent flap 1 cm (⅜ in) towards the wrong side, and secure it in place with a slip stitch. See page 166 for how to slip stitch.

3. On the left back piece, fold the vent flap towards the right side and sew a horizontal seam where the folded edge of the hem will be. Trim off the excess fabric as shown in the picture. Turn right side out and press.

4. Place the right and left back pieces right sides together, and sew the centre back seam. As you approach the vent flaps, sew them together along the diagonal line. Press the seam open until you reach the corner where the seam continues diagonally. Clip a small notch in the seam allowance on the right back piece to allow for pressing the seam allowance upwards along the diagonal line.

5. Turn the garment right side out. You will see the left back piece overlaps the right at the vent. Press the vent to lie flat. Sew a diagonal line of stitching over the vent from the centre back seam down to the edge of the vent flap, as shown in the picture.

[1]

[3]

[4]

[5]

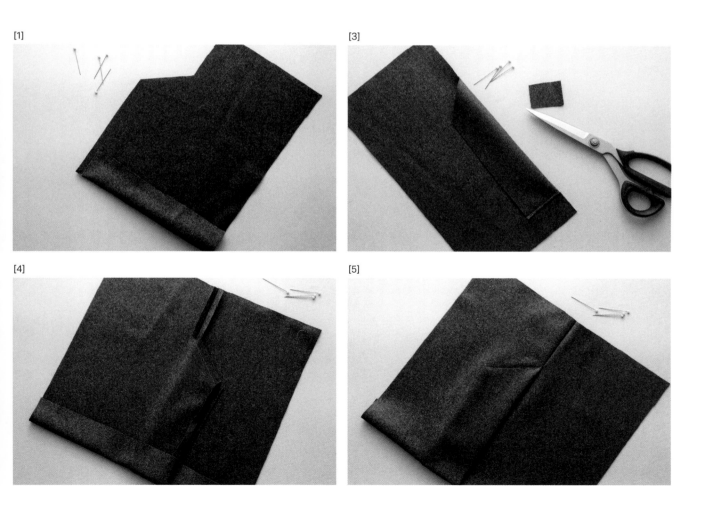

Fashion trends change quickly: one moment everyone wants big puff sleeves and voluminous ruffle edges, and the next moment the trend is clean, straight lines with minimal extras. Our personal taste is also highly variable, and wearing clothes that reflect who we are is an excellent way to show more personality. We hope this book will be suitable for everyone and remain equally relevant year after year, so we have dedicated a separate section to variations that can be made to the patterns. Here we will show you how to easily add details or make changes to the pattern pieces in the book to give your clothes their own expression and design.

Variations

Ruffles are nice details that can be added to create a more exciting look. For example, you can add a ruffle to the bottom of a skirt to create more volume or add ruffles to armholes and trouser (pants) hems. You can use this method to add ruffles wherever you desire.

Ruffles and gathers

1. Measure along the edge where you want to add the ruffle.

2. Multiply this measurement by 2 to determine the length of the ruffle. Depending on the desired fullness, you can choose a higher number for a more voluminous ruffle or a lower number for a subtler effect. This measurement will be referred to as measurement A.

3. Decide on the desired height of the ruffle. This is measurement B.

4. Cut a rectangular piece of fabric that measures A x B. Hem the bottom edge, and secure any raw edges with a zigzag stitch or overlock. Sew the short edges together, right side facing.

   Note! If you are adding ruffles along a non-circular edge, do not sew the short sides together. Instead, fold them to the wrong side and sew in place.

5. Sew gathering stitches along the long side without the hem, adjust the length of the ruffle as required to fit, and sew it to the garment. See page 188 for how to gather.

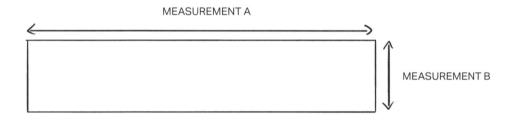

MEASUREMENT A

MEASUREMENT B

Pockets are not just a practical utility, but can also lift the design of a garment and give it a new look. For instance, adding patch pockets to a pair of trousers (pants) will give them a more rugged and expressive appearance. Here we will demonstrate some different kinds of pockets to experiment with on your projects.

Pockets

In-seam pocket

You can create an invisible pocket by drawing a bean-shaped pocket, which you sew into the side seam of the garment. This can be done for most types of garment and is practical to have in trousers, skirts and jackets.
Important! The pocket must be placed before sewing the side seam.

1. Cut the pocket pieces in your chosen fabric – you need two pieces per pocket.

2. Mark the opening where you want to place the pockets in the side seam of the garment.

3. Place one pocket piece, right sides together, aligned over the side seam of the front of the garment. Sew in place with a 1 cm (⅜ in) seam allowance. Repeat on the back of the garment.

4. Press the pocket piece towards the seam allowance (so away from the garment) and sew through the pocket piece and the seam allowance only.

5. Place the front and back pieces with the pockets, right sides together. Sew the side seam and pocket in one piece by sewing the side seam from the top of the garment, then sewing around the outer edge of the pocket piece, then the remaining side seam down to the bottom of the garment.

6. Press the seam to the side and press the pocket bag towards the front of the garment. From the right side, the pocket is neatly concealed.

[1]

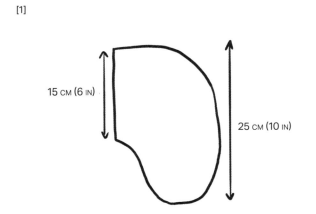

15 cm (6 in)

25 cm (10 in)

[3]

[5]

[6]

Patch pocket

Patch pockets are attached to the outside of a garment and can have a variety of shapes and styles. Here are some suggestions for different pocket shapes and how to achieve a result that is both solid and looks good.

1. Start by drawing the pocket in the desired size and shape and cut it out of paper. Place the paper pocket on the garment to see if the size and design match.

2. Cut the pocket out of the fabric. Add 1 cm (⅜ in) seam allowance around the edges, and 3 cm (1¼ in) along the top opening.

3. Secure the raw edges with a zigzag or overlock stitch. Fold all the edges 1 cm (⅜ in) towards the wrong side and press all around the pocket. Then fold the top opening edge over by another 2 cm (¾ in) to conceal the raw edge within the fold.

4. Topstitch from the right side along the opening of the pocket to hold the fold in place.

5. Pin the pocket to the garment and sew it in place from the right side around the sides and bottom. Try to sew as close to the folded edge as possible.

6. You can reinforce the pocket by topstitching a parallel seam line within the first seam or sewing a decorative rectangle or triangle at the top of each corner.

[1]

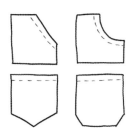

[4]

[6]

Pocket flap

Pocket flaps are a stylish detail that can be used over a patch pocket. The flap can be fastened with a button and buttonhole, snap fasteners, or just loosely laid over the pocket. Here's how to make a pocket flap:

1. Draw the pocket flap on paper in the same way as you did for the patch pocket. Make sure it is slightly wider than the pocket itself, about 1 cm (⅜ in) is sufficient.

2. Cut the pocket flap x 2 in fabric, adding a 1 cm (⅜ in) seam allowance all around.

3. Place the pieces right sides together and sew along the edges, but leave the top edge open.

4. Trim the seam allowance and corners and turn the flap right out. Fold the top edges inward by 1 cm (⅜ in) encasing all the raw edges inside the fabric layers and press.

5. Topstitch around the sides and bottom edges, excluding the top edge.

6. Pin the pocket flap over the pocket on the garment. You can decide the placement based on what looks best. Ensure that the flap overlaps the pocket sufficiently, allowing room for attaching a fastening if desired.

7. Topstitch in place from the right side along the top edge. Secure well at the corners. Backstitch at the beginning and the end to secure the seam properly.

[3]

[5]

[7]

Welt pocket

A welt pocket is inserted into the centre of a pattern piece, for example in the front of a jacket or coat. It is a stylish detail that requires precision. All the parts you need to sew a welt pocket are on the pattern sheet. You will need pattern pieces for the pocket bag and pocket flap; the pocket bag should be cut as one long and one short piece (ending at the dotted line on the pattern sheet). Here we show you how to sew a single welt pocket, as used for the coat, or a welt pocket with a flap over the opening, as used for the blazer.

1.

Transfer the pocket markings from the pattern onto the front of the garment. The marking shows the centreline; you should also draw a parallel line 1 cm (⅜ in) above and 1 cm (⅜ in) below the centreline, which corresponds to the seam lines.

Iron interfacing onto the wrong side of the fabric where the pocket opening will be, and also mark on this side.

[1]

[3]

Welt pocket with flap

Single welt pocket

2. Iron interfacing onto the pocket flap and fold it in half lengthwise, right sides together. Sew down the short sides. Clip the seam allowance at the corners, turn the flap right side out and press it from the right side. Tack (baste) along the raw edge to close the opening. Cut the corners off diagonally above the tacking stitches.

3. **Welt pocket with flap**
With the front of the garment facing you, place the flap above the centreline, aligning the raw edge of the flap with the centreline.

Sew the flap in place along the line marked above the centreline.

Single welt pocket
With the front of the garment facing you, place the flap below the centreline, aligning the raw edge of the flap with the centreline.

Sew the flap in place along the line marked below the centreline.

[4]

[5]

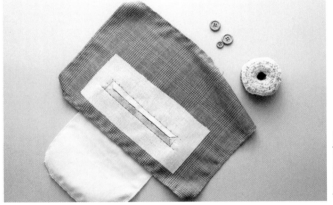

Welt pocket with flap

Single welt pocket

4. Place the longest pocket bag, right sides together, over the pocket marking. The straight raw edge should point downward and overlap the lower line by 1 cm (⅜ in). The flap is now sandwiched between the front of the garment and the pocket piece for the welt pocket with flap, but will show above the pocket piece on the single welt pocket.

5. Turn the garment wrong side up and use short stitches to sew a long rectangle along the outer marked lines. Then carefully cut through all layers along the centreline. Stop 1 cm (⅜ in) from each end and clip diagonally towards each corner to form a Y-shape on each side. Be careful not to cut through the stitches.

6. Turn the pocket bag through the slit you cut in step 5 so that it is now on the wrong side of the front piece. Gently pull the small triangles on the short sides to square the opening. Press well.

7. Place the short pocket piece on the pocket piece that is already attached, right sides together, so that the straight edges are aligned. Stitch along the straight edge with a 1 cm (⅜ in) seam allowance, and then around the entire pocket. Attach the small triangles to the pocket piece, making sure you do not sew through any layers other than the pocket pieces and triangles.

8. **Welt pocket with flap**
Turn the garment right side up. The flap will now be folded down over the pocket opening. Press with an iron and stitch along the top edge of the flap to hold it in place.

Single welt pocket
Turn the garment right side up. The flap should be folded upward over the pocket opening to form the single welt. Press and stitch along each short side to hold the welt in place.

[7]

[8]

Welt pocket with flap

Single welt pocket

You can easily add a decorative collar to a neckline by drawing a collar based on the top pattern and neckline you have chosen.

Decorative collar

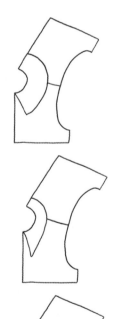

1. Fold down the shoulder seam allowance at the front and back top pattern pieces, and align the shoulders.

2. Take a transparent sheet, such as tracing paper, and lay it over the pattern pieces. Draw the desired shape of the collar along the neckline. Remember to add a seam allowance along the outer edge.

3. Cut out four collar pieces from your fabric. If your neckline is wide enough and doesn't require an opening at the back, you can cut the collar pieces on the fold at the centre back, reducing the number to two collar pieces.

4. As an option, you can reinforce the underside of the collar piece with interfacing for added stability and structure.

5. Place pairs of collar pieces right sides together and sew around all the outer edges, but leave the neckline edge open.

6. Trim the seam allowance and corners, then turn the collar right side out. Press well. You can also topstitch from the right side along the outer edge.

7. When attaching the neckline facing, place the collar right side up, between the neckline and the facing and sew it in place through all layers.

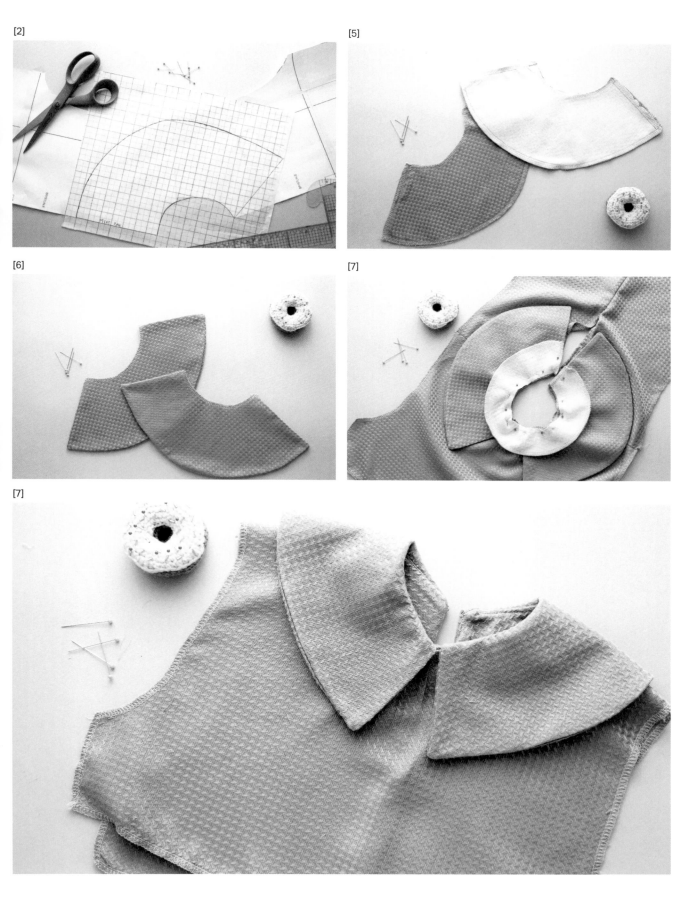

Create your own tie bands or belts to elegantly cinch the waist of dresses and skirts, adding style and silhouette to the garments featured in the book.

Tie bands and belts

Tie bands

To create a tie band, cut a fabric strip that is at least 10 cm (4 in) wide and twice as long as your waist measurement. If necessary, you can join two shorter strips together at the short ends.

1. Fold the fabric strip in half right sides together and cut across diagonally at each end.

2. Sew the short ends and one long side of the fabric with a seam allowance of 1 cm (⅜ in), making sure to leave a 5 cm (2 in) gap in the centre of the long side. Trim the corners of the seam allowance.

3. Turn the tie band right side out through the opening. Use a knitting needle to pick out the corners.

4. Press the tie band flat, ensuring the raw edges of the opening are folded and concealed on the inside of the tie. Topstitch around the entire tie band, about 0.5 cm (¼ in) in from the edge.

[1]

[2]

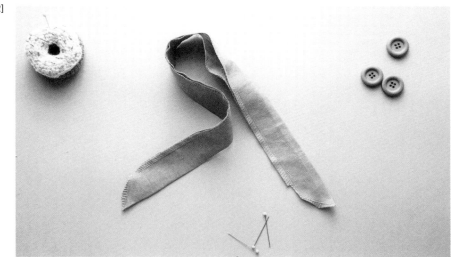

[4]

Belt

To create a belt, cut two fabric strips that are 6 cm (2⅜ in) and as long as the circumference where you want the belt to sit, plus an additional 25 cm (10 in). Cut the same measurements in interfacing as well.

1. Iron interfacing onto the wrong side of both belt pieces. Place them right sides together and sew around the entire edge, leaving about 5 cm (2 in) open on one long side. Trim all corners of the seam allowance.

2. Turn the belt right side out through the opening. Use a knitting needle to pick out the corners.

3. Press the belt flat, ensuring the raw edges of the opening are folded and concealed on the inside of the tie. Topstitch around the entire belt, about 0.5 cm (¼ in) from the edge.

4. Attach a belt buckle to one end of the belt. If your buckle requires holes, check if your sewing machine has the ability to sew eyelets. Otherwise, you can use metal eyelets. Try on the belt to check how tight you want it to fit and fasten it at the innermost hole.

[1]

[3]

[4]

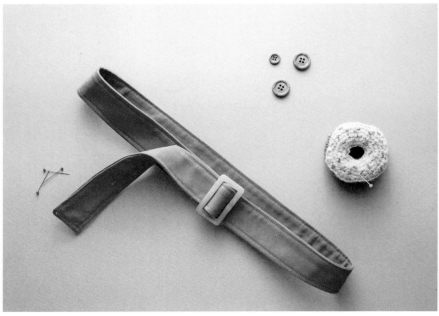

Belt loops

To make five belt loops, each 10 cm (4 in) long, cut out a fabric strip that measures 50 cm x 3 cm (20 in x 1¼ in). If your fabric is thin, consider ironing interfacing onto the wrong side for added stability.

1. Finish the long sides by either overlocking (serging) or using a zigzag stitch. Fold one side of the strip 1 cm (⅜ in) towards the wrong side and press. Repeat this step on the other side. The fabric strip is now folded into three layers.

2. Topstitch along each long side of the fabric strip, sewing as close to the folded edge as possible while ensuring you catch all three layers.

3. Cut the strip into five equal pieces, each approximately 10 cm (4 in) long.

4. Position the belt loops on your trouser or skirt waistband: place two loops in the front, two at the side seam on the back piece, and one in the centre back, or adjust the placement as desired to best suit your project.

Tip! *You can follow the same procedure to make belt loops for attaching to the side seam of a dress to hold the tie band in place. In that case, you only need a 20 cm (8 in) long fabric strip.*

[1]

[2]

[3]

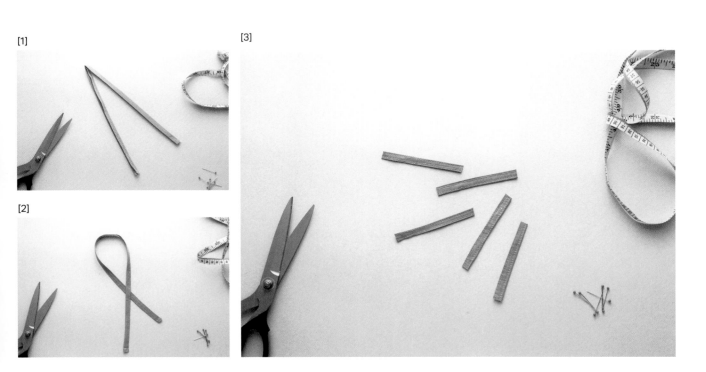

An alternative to using a cuff to finish wide sleeves is to make an elastic casing at the bottom of the sleeve. Extend the length of the pattern piece where you want to add the casing by the width of your elastic plus 1.5 cm (⅝ in). For example, if your elastic is 1-cm (⅜-in) wide, extend the pattern piece by 2.5 cm (1 in) at the end where you'll insert the elastic casing, such as at the sleeve's bottom.

Elastic casing

1. Fold the bottom edge of the sleeve 1 cm (⅜ in) towards the wrong side and press.

2. Then fold it again towards the wrong side, creating a casing wide enough to accommodate the elastic, with approximately 0.5 cm (¼ in) of extra space. For example, if you added a 2.5 cm (1 in) casing extension, the folded casing should be 1.5 cm (⅝ in) wide. Pin along the folded edge.

3. Topstitch along the folded top edge to create the casing, leaving an opening large enough to thread the elastic through.

4. Attach a safety pin to one end of the elastic and thread it through the casing and remove the safety pin.

5. Ensure that the elastic is not twisted inside the casing. Overlap the ends of the elastic and sew them back and forth a few times to secure them. Once the elastic is in place, close the opening in the casing with a few stitches by hand.

Tip! *To determine the appropriate length of elastic, wrap it around your body where the casing will be placed and adjust it to a comfortable fit before cutting.*

[3]

[4]

[5]

Here we demonstrate how you can use the base sleeve patterns to achieve a variety of sleeve variations – these techniques can be used for both straight and fitted sleeves. By using the marked lines on the pattern sheet, you can easily divide the sleeve into several parts and use them to create a sleeve with more width. The illustrations and instructions here describe how to create the various sleeve types. We have defined some standard measurements as a starting point for the different designs, but the same principle can be used to create sleeves with both more and less volume. Feel free to experiment with this if you want a slightly different look.

Sleeve variations

Balloon sleeve

Leg of mutton sleeve

Short puff sleeve

Combined sleeve

Balloon sleeve

To create a balloon sleeve, you will also need to attach a cuff at the bottom of the sleeve. On the pattern sheet, you will find a cuff for your size.

1. Fold the cuff lengthwise, wrong sides together, and press. Then, unfold the cuff and press one long edge 1 cm (⅜ in) towards the wrong side.

2. Sew gathering stitches along the lower edge of both sleeves and gather the fabric to match the width of the cuff. See page 184 for how to gather.

3. Attach the bottom edge of the sleeve to the unfolded edge of the cuff, right sides together, and sew to secure the gathers in place. Press the seam allowance towards the sleeve.

4. Lay the top with right side facing up and attach the sleeve to the armhole.

5. Place the top right sides together and sew the side seam from the bottom of the cuff, under the armhole, and to the bottom of the top. Press the seam open.

6. Fold the cuff over to the wrong side and sew the folded edge to the seam allowance between the sleeve and the cuff. Remove the gathering stitches.

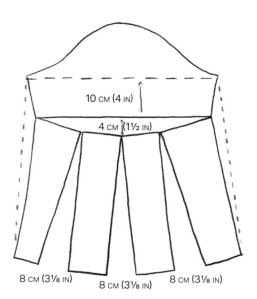

10 cm (4 in)

4 cm (1½ in)

8 cm (3⅛ in)   8 cm (3⅛ in)   8 cm (3⅛ in)

Draw the pattern piece for the sleeve on pattern paper and cut it out. On the pattern piece: Draw a horizontal line parallel to the armhole and 10 cm (4 in) below. First cut along the vertical lines marked on the pattern piece from the lower edge up to the new line you have just drawn. Then cut along the horizontal line, so that the lower part of the sleeve now consists of four pieces. Place all the pieces on a piece of pattern paper and spread the four lower pieces apart according to the measurements indicated in the illustration. The measurements are indicative and can be adjusted for desired volume (larger measurements provide more volume). Draw the outer edges of the pattern piece onto the pattern paper below, ending with a new pattern piece for a balloon sleeve.

Leg of mutton sleeve

1. Sew gathering threads along the sleeve cap and gather the fabric together to fit the circumference of the armhole.

2. Place the top with the right side facing you and sew the sleeve to the armhole. Remove the gathering threads.

3. Place the top right sides together and sew the side seam from the bottom of the sleeve, under the armhole and down to the bottom of the top. Press the seams open.

4. Fold up a small hem at the bottom of the sleeve. Topstitch around the fold.

Draw a pattern piece for the sleeve on pattern paper and cut it out. First, cut the pattern piece along the vertical lines marked on the pattern piece from the top edge down to the elbow line. Then cut along the elbow line so the upper part of the sleeve now consists of four pieces. Place all the pieces on a new piece of pattern paper and spread the four top pieces out according to the measurements shown in the illustration. The measurements are indicative and can be adjusted for desired volume (larger measurements provide more volume). Draw the outer edges of the pattern piece on the pattern paper underneath, ending up with a new pattern piece for a leg of mutton sleeve.

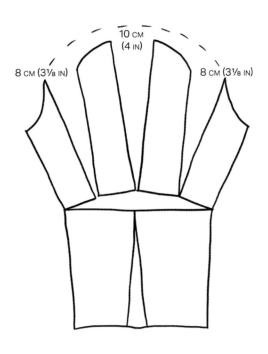

10 CM (4 IN)

8 CM (3⅛ IN)

8 CM (3⅛ IN)

Short puff sleeve

You can make a short puff sleeve by cutting the sleeve at the elbow line. Sew gathering threads along the top of the sleeve and fold up a small hem at the bottom edge of the sleeve.

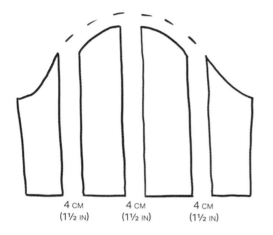

4 CM
(1½ IN) 4 CM
(1½ IN) 4 CM
(1½ IN)

Draw the pattern piece for the sleeve on pattern paper, ending the sleeve at the elbow line, and cut it out. Cut along the vertical lines marked on the pattern piece from top to bottom, resulting in four separate parts. Arrange these parts on a new piece of pattern paper, spacing them out according to the measurements in the illustration. The measurements are approximate and can be adjusted to achieve the desired volume. Trace the outline of the pattern piece onto the underlying pattern paper, creating a new pattern piece for the short puff sleeve.

Combined sleeve

To create a striking statement sleeve, you can combine a puff sleeve and a balloon sleeve to achieve fullness both at the top and bottom of the sleeve. You will use the techniques for both puff and balloon sleeves, by sewing gathering threads at both the top and bottom of the sleeve, and attaching a cuff at the bottom edge.

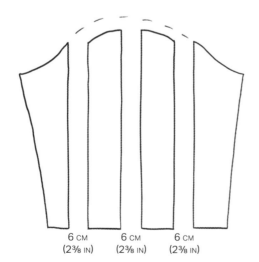

6 CM
(2⅜ IN) 6 CM
(2⅜ IN) 6 CM
(2⅜ IN)

Draw the pattern piece for the sleeve on pattern paper and cut it out. Cut along the vertical lines marked on the pattern piece from top to bottom resulting in four separate sections. Arrange these sections on a new piece of pattern paper, spacing them out according to the measurements in the illustration. These measurements are approximate and can be adjusted to achieve the desired level of volume. Trace the outer edges of the pattern piece onto the pattern paper, creating a new pattern piece that combines the elements of a puff sleeve and a balloon sleeve.

You can create different necklines by drawing your desired shape on the pattern piece and creating a corresponding facing, as explained on page 174. The illustrations below show examples of classic necklines, but you can also experiment with your own designs. If you change the length of the shoulder on the front piece, remember to make a corresponding change to the back piece so the shoulder seams match up.

Neckline

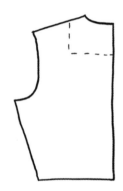

Square neckline

V-shape neckline

Deeper neckline

In many of the patterns, you have the option to adjust the length of the garments. You can easily make these adjustments on the pattern pieces using the reference lines provided. Remember that when modifying the length, you should always add an extra amount for the hem allowance.

Adjusting the length

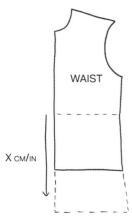

Top

To change the length of a top, start with marking the waist. Measure how long you want the garment to be from the waist and transfer this to the pattern piece. When transferring to the pattern, start from the centre front edge and lengthen or shorten this accordingly. Once you have changed the length here on the pattern, draw a line at 90-degrees from the end point to mark the bottom of the pattern piece. Then, extend the side seam to meet this line at the bottom of the pattern piece. By doing it this way, you can angle the side seam outwards correctly.

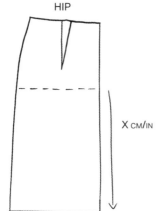

Skirt

For a skirt there is a marking for the hip. Locate the hip marking as a starting reference for length adjustments. Measure from the hip to determine the desired length of the garment and transfer this measurement onto the pattern piece.

Acknowledgements

We are grateful for the opportunity to share this book, and want to thank all the people who have helped make it a reality. Ida Bjørvik has photographed all the outfits and really made the clothes shine and ourselves look and feel our best. Axel Berggraf Egenæs is a true design virtuoso who made our vision come true in the layout process. Oreolu, Harriet and Ann Kristin, our wonderful editors, have supported us and been great partners in making this book its best version.

MeterMeter and Lillestrøm Sysenter enabled us to work with beautiful fabrics during the design process, sponsoring us with materials for the following garments:.

MeterMeter
Green turtleneck dress, blue turtleneck sweater, yellow blouse, beige wrap skirt, green crewneck, white T-shirt, green T-shirt, white everyday dress, purple wrap dress, green jumpsuit, pink jumpsuit.

Lillestrøm Sysenter
Beige trousers, blue blazer, beige blazer, both the coats, beige blazer, skirt in faux leather, blue everyday dress, pink babydoll dress.

About the authors

Oda
I've always been fascinated by craftsmanship. When I became serious about sewing, my goal was to create the clothing I dreamt of wearing myself but, for various reasons, couldn't always find. I realized I could bring these visions to life from home, with a needle, thread, fabric and a vision – and got hooked on the amazing freedom and satisfaction that came with this feeling of mastery and the possibilities it opened up. Today it is my great joy to share this passion through my business and Instagram profile, Flid (@flid.no), where I create and sell sewing patterns and made-to-order garments.
My love for romantic and feminine designs, rooted in contemporary and structured shapes, is at the centre of the fashion I create, hoping to inspire more to embrace the sewing machine and its endless possibilities.

Kristin
My passion for clothing and fashion started at a young age. For as long as I can remember, I've been invested in what I wear and always had a love for clothes that stand out and add that little extra. In addition, I've always been fond of exploring creativity and making things. A few years ago I received my first sewing machine as a birthday present, and then everything fell into place. I was immediately hooked on sewing my own clothes, and since then I've spent countless hours in front of the sewing machine. I love that I can use my creativity to make garments that nobody else has, and find that nothing beats the feeling of wearing clothes that you've designed and sewn yourself. Since learning how to sew, I've been a finalist in the Norwegian edition of *The Sewing Bee* in 2019 and share my projects through my Instagram account @vaag.oslo.

Fabric quantity guide

Basic foundation pattern	Included in calculation	34	36	38	40	42	44	46	48	50
UK size		6	8	10	12	14	16	18	20	22
US size		2	4	6	8	10	12	14	16	18
Straight top	Front piece, back piece, sleeve	1.3 m (1½ yd)	1.3 m (1½ yd)	1.3 m (1½ yd)	1.3 m (1½ yd)	1.5 m (1¾ yd)	1.5 m (1¾ yd)	1.5 m (1¾ yd)	1.5 m (1¾ yd)	1.8 m (2 yd)
Fitted top	Front piece, back piece, sleeve	1 m (1⅛ yd)	1 m (1⅛ yd)	1 m (1⅛ yd)	1.2 m (1⅓ yd)	1.2 m (1⅓ yd)	1.2 m (1⅓ yd)	1.2 m (1⅓ yd)	1.3 m (1½ yd)	1.3 m (1½ yd)
Skirt	Front piece, back piece, waistband	1 m (1⅛ yd)	1 m (1⅛ yd)	1 m (1⅛ yd)	1.2 m (1⅓ yd)	1.2 m (1⅓ yd)	1.2 m (1⅓ yd)	1.2 m (1⅓ yd)	1.3 m (1½ yd)	1.3 m (1½ yd)
Trousers	Front piece, back piece, waistband	1.8 m (2 yd)	1.8 m (2 yd)	2 m (2¼ yd)	2 m (2¼ yd)	2 m (2¼ yd)	2.2 m (2½ yd)	2.2 m (2½ yd)	2.3 m (2⅝ yd)	2.3 m (2⅝ yd)
Jacket	Front piece, back piece, collar, sleeve, pocket flap, pocket	1.5 m (1¾ yd)	1.5 m (1¾ yd)	1.5 m (1¾ yd)	1.8 m (2 yd)	1.8 m (2 yd)	2 m (2¼ yd)	2.2 m (2½ yd)	2.2 m (2½ yd)	2.2 m (2½ yd)
Swimsuit	Front piece, back piece	1.2 m (1⅓ yd)	1.2 m (1⅓ yd)	1.2 m (1⅓ yd)	1.2 m (1⅓ yd)	1.2 m (1⅓ yd)	1.2 m (1⅓ yd)	1.3 m (1½ yd)	1.3 m (1½ yd)	1.3 m (1½ yd)
Baguette bag	Side piece, bottom, ring tab, handle	0.5 m (⅝ yd)								

These measurements are based on fabric with a 140 cm (55 in) width.

First published as *Flid – sy tidløse garderobeklassikere* in 2021
by Gyldendal Norsk Forlag AS

This English language edition published in 2023
by Quadrille, an imprint of Hardie Grant Publishing

Quadrille
52–54 Southwark Street
London SE1 1UN
quadrille.com

Managing Director Sarah Lavelle
Senior Commissioning Editor Harriet Butt
Assistant Editor Oreolu Grillo
Translator Elisabeth Stray Gausel
Copy Editor Marie Clayton
Proofreader Katie Hardwicke
Designers Axel Berggraf Egenæs, Alicia House
Photographers Ida Bjørvik, Oda Stormoen, Kristin Vaag
Illustrator Kristin Vaag
Head of Production Stephen Lang
Production Controller Martina Georgieva

Cataloguing in Publication Data: a catalogue record for this book is
available from the British Library.

Text © Gyldendal Norsk Forlag AS/Oda Stormoen & Kristin Vaag 2023
Design © Quadrille 2023
Photography © Ida Bjørvik 2023 except for pages 14, 16, 24, 29, 164–195
    and 201–215 Oda Stormoen & Kristin Vaag 2023
Patterns © Oda Stormoen 2023

ISBN 978 1 83783 108 1

Printed in China using soy inks

FSC
www.fsc.org

MIX
Paper from
responsible sources
FSC™ C020056